AMERICA EXPLAINED

A GUIDE FOR INDIAN IMMIGRANTS

ALLISON SINGH

D1089313

For my Family

1

STARTING THE CONVERSATION

Imagine we find ourselves sitting side by side on a flight from India to America. Perhaps the flight is from New Delhi to New York, the familiar route traveled by so many Indian immigrants, including those in my family. We smile politely and take our seats, settling in for the long flight. I wonder if you want to talk. I hope you do.

Think of this book as the conversation between us. We start with the simple facts - where we are going and why - and then, as others slip on headphones, we share more. We tell each other what it is *really* like to live in our home country. Not what we see in movies or television - we know those are extremes and stereotypes. We share stories of everyday life, and through those stories we see the reality of living in another land.

I know you have questions about the real America, because I have been answering them for my family and friends for years. Likewise, as the curious white girl in a big Indian family, I ask my relatives everything from the difference between *mami* and *chachi* to when touching feet is and isn't appropriate. These are kitchen conversations over cups of *chai*, since it is impossible to talk over the blaring Bollywood music at most parties. I love my Indian family, and it is from that love that this book was born.

I've seen relatives achieve great success in America who were too shy to answer the phone when they first arrived. I grew close to one cousin because she was too afraid to talk to some of our older, more established family members. With me, she had nothing to lose. We laughed when we made silly mistakes - me with Hindi words, she with English. We cried when we realized a lost piece of mail and simple mistake on an immigration form meant her husband's arrival from India would be delayed another year and his place in a residency program was at risk. She told me that our conversations made her feel welcome in this country, less scared, and confident that she could actually make it here.

The truth is she would have made it whether or not she met me. But the possibility that my words could make her feel more welcome - that struck me, especially in today's political climate where immigration is talked about as a "problem" and not one of America's greatest strengths. Instead of judging immigrants, how about we try to make them feel more welcome? It's what any polite host would do. If someone came to your home, would you assume they knew where to find the bathroom, or whether to take off their shoes? Americans are not giving enough guidance, and too many of us are closing our doors.

I've heard from too many Indian immigrants that for the first time they feel unwelcome in America. I want to tell you that America is a land of immigrants, and you are not only welcome, but needed here. The truth many Americans do not acknowledge is that without immigrants, our country would not be as "great" as it is. My goal with this book is to use my words to somehow, maybe, make the transition from India to America a little easier for you. Perhaps my words can make this land a little less unknown, so that you can make it your own.

So let's get started.

About this Book

This book can be read out of order. It is organized into chapters with sets of questions. Skip to the chapters or questions most relevant to you.

I've tried to write about the immigrant experience from different points of view. I interviewed doctors, of course, since medicine is a common entryway to America for Indians. But I also interviewed teachers, programmers, business owners, accountants, physical therapists, corporate executives and pharmacists, among others. I spoke with parents and singles, arranged and love matches, and generations from the trailblazers of the 1970's to the newest immigrants.

Still, I have much to learn about the immigrant experience and what it means to be Indian in America. After all, I'm white and born here, so there is a limit to what I can learn and pass on. However, I soon realized that being white gives me an advantage because I hear things that would never be said around non-white people. I share some of this with you throughout the book.

This book is the first edition of what will be an annual publication. So please tell me what I got wrong and what I missed. Tell me what you think others should know. To send me questions and comments and sign up for updates and special offers, please email me at allisonsinghbooks@gmail.com or visit my website allisonsingh.com. You can find pictures related to the book on Instagram at @americaexplainedbookseries, and articles on the Facebook page America Explained Book Series.

My Immigrant Family

The diversity of America is true for my family as well. Three of my grandparents arrived in New York City as immigrants in the early twentieth century, two from Italy, one from Scotland. The fourth is the daughter of a woman who traveled alone from Ireland at the age of sixteen. Their stories of bravery, grit and sacrifice are the lifeblood of our family history. Both grandfathers fought in World War II. My Irish great-grandfather returned from World War I with mustard gas poisoning and lived the remainder of his life in a veteran's hospital.

I continued this tradition by marrying a first-generation Indian immigrant (he was born here, making him "first generation"). My husband's family is from Patna, Bihar, a very poor region of India. His parents came to America in 1973 after his father was offered a medical fellowship from a hospital in Queens, New York. His father was denied career advancement in India because of his caste, just as he had been denied the first spot in his medical school class for the same reason. His grades placed him first, but a group from a higher caste objected to giving him the top rank. Coming to America was a good way to learn advanced medical skills and wait until those blocking his advancement retired. He told me he checked with sources back home regularly to see if this happened.

My mother-in-law did not like America at first. She was unaccustomed to the cold, the customs and the loneliness. She held a Masters of English Literature from India, but did not have the certification to teach in America, and was too timid to face an American classroom. She told me her husband had his colleagues at the hospital to learn from, but all she had was television shows like Golden Girls and The Young and the Restless.

She had a child, which helped her loneliness. My father-in-law became comfortable in America, and realized the potential for wealth that was not possible in India. They had a baby, brought over their two children from India, moved to Long Island and began their life as a family of five in America.

During that time, their house was known as "Ellis Island" after the iconic destination for immigrants arriving in New York by ship in the nineteenth and twentieth centuries. The nickname stuck because my husband's parents sponsored so many family members and their house was home base while these relatives found their way. My husband remembers losing his room to the latest arrival, and sharing his bed with loving aunties and snoring uncles. The house was busy as family members worked odd jobs and studied. When he had time, my father-in-law taught his nieces and nephews about money, investing and driving in America.

For two people from such different backgrounds, my husband and I met in a very common way - at college. At the time, the idea of a white daughter-in-law had to be a nightmare for my mother-in-law. Through mutual respect and love, we are now very close.

I live between cultures and try to create a blended culture for my children. I consider myself fortunate to have a dual perspective - born to a family of pre-war European immigrants, married into a family of recent (and continuing) immigration from India. I see commonalities where others may not.

To me, immigration is inspiring, challenging and fun. I'll never forget taking a new immigrant to the ocean for the first time, or watching election results with a political junkie Indian here on a visitor visa (who knew more about American politics than most people in the room). It's these small moments, the humanity and love, that we need to remember when we discuss immigration. America is connected to the rest of the world through these bonds. I can't think of a stronger national resource than that.

2

I'M HERE...NOW WHAT?

On the whole, Americans are welcoming people. You may find us ignorant about the world beyond our borders. Many of us live in a safe and comfortable bubble created by our geographic location and abundance of riches. But like a real bubble, the American one can pop with a gentle touch.

My advice is to approach any American ignorance with curiosity and a willingness to share your culture. Just because Americans never had to think about some of the issues common to Indians doesn't mean we are closed to learning about them. Give us a chance - we might surprise you. As one Indian immigrant described it, Americans don't know how lucky they are. She doesn't blame us or even think this is a negative. She understands our assumptions about the world, and our reactions when we learn the truth.

I ended each interview for this book with the question: What is the main thing you want Indian immigrants to know about America? Here is what the interviewees said:

"It's not like the movies, where money comes easily and people don't have to work hard. You are not here just to have a good time.

It takes hard work to succeed in America. There is a lot of competition, you will not have as much help as you had at home, and things are much more expensive."

"Be flexible and ready to adapt. You might have to change some things, but if you have decided to come to America, you should be willing to make some changes."

"It is harder than it looks in the movies - much harder."

"Go out and be with people. This is really the only way to learn the customs. Don't be afraid to make mistakes and be embarrassed sometimes. Most Americans are open to learning and helping immigrants."

"In America, you are going to be a minority in a majority white country. Understanding race history and race relations will help."

"It is still true that in America you can make it if you work hard. You will hear a lot of Americans say this is not true, but in many ways this is because America has become a society of entitlement. If you keep your mind on work and not entitlement, you will succeed and be much happier."

"Knowing English and familiarity with English idioms, slang and conversation is the main reason I could succeed here. I attended English schools in India, but I also watched a lot of American movies. These shows introduced me to the types of people I would meet in America - such as Hispanics and black people - and how they spoke. I was also familiar with the cop cars, skyscraper buildings. Of course America is not like the movies, but as far as communication watching these movies helped."

"The educated Americans are the greatest people."

"Feel free to ask questions. In India, you may have held back and not asked questions. In America, people are friendly and happy to help. I came when I was fourteen and made a friend before I even knew the language. We are still in touch and joke about it now."

"Learn the language so you feel comfortable speaking to anyone and anywhere."

"Be careful when you speak. You can get in trouble for what you say here. People are easily offended and one mistake can ruin your career."

"Watch American sports, the news and television shows so you can understand the culture and be able to talk to work colleagues, patients and friends."

3

A WORD ON THE "AMERICAN DREAM"

The "American Dream" is one of those phrases that we grow up with in America, and often accept without challenge.

The truth is there is no one definition of the American dream - the American experience is as diverse as its people. Not everyone who comes to America has a dream, and that's okay. Many immigrants travel to America with mixed emotions, wishing they could pursue their dreams back home. They leave behind family, friends and a sense of place and belonging. Yet they know that pursuing their dreams at home is not possible because of barriers such as violence, lack of jobs or systems of favoritism and corruption. America offers a chance to overcome those obstacles, but there is a cost that Americans born here often do not see.

Some come because they have no choice. They may be sent by an employer, or following a spouse. Maybe they don't want to be the next immigrant success story, the new Silicon Valley billionaire. Maybe they wish they could raise their children with the comforts of home, surrounded by family and a familiar culture.

This book is for everyone. I write for those who see America as a fresh start, and for those who come unwillingly and just hope to survive. I write for those who desire to fit in, those fearful of losing their identity, and those trying to balance both.

There is no one way to "be" an American. Arriving with mixed feelings does not make you less American. Missing home does not undermine your loyalty to America. My mother-in-law told me that soon after her arrival she was asked if she felt American or Indian. She honestly felt both, but was afraid to say it. Now, she feels American, but back then, she still felt Indian. It's a process, not a switch that can be turned when your plane lands in New York.

Regardless of where you are in the process, we need all voices heard in America, especially today. Don't be afraid to speak your truth.

4

WHO IS AN AMERICAN, REALLY?

*A*ren't all Americans immigrants?*

A cousin of ours once asked my husband, "Why do they call us (Indians) foreigners when everyone comes to America from someplace else?" America is a land of immigrants. There is no denying it. The only non-immigrants are the Native Americans, also called "Indians" (more on this later).

So when did immigrants come to America, and from where? Below is a brief summary of the major waves of immigration in U.S. history.

Brief Outline of Immigration to U.S.

1500's - European immigration from Spain and France

1600's - British immigration; America claimed as colony of the British empire.

1600 - 1619 - First slaves arrive in America, brought by Dutch slave traders

1815-1850 - European immigration from Ireland (famine), Germany and Asia (to west coast, gold rush)

1882 - Congress adopts the Chinese Exclusion Act - first federal limit on immigration

1880's -1920 - Immigration from Central, Eastern and Southern Europe

1917 - Immigration Act of 1917 - Restricted immigration from Asia. Only immigrants passing a "literacy test" were allowed to stay in the U.S. (passed over veto by President Woodrow Wilson).

1924 - Congress limits immigration to 2% of the nationality existing in the U.S. as of 1890. This policy favored Western Europeans and limited immigration from Eastern Europe and Asia.

Post-1945 - After World War II, U.S. allowed entry for refugees from Europe, the USSR and Cuba.

1965 - Congress ends immigration quotas. Quotas had favored European immigrants. Americans could now sponsor relatives from their country of origin for citizenship.

Post-1965 - Rise in immigration from Asia and Latin America.

What is the "melting pot"?

The melting pot is about assimilation. The idea is that our individual identity is somehow "melted" into a shared American cultural identity. The tricky part is balancing assimilation into American culture with preserving your own culture.

My grandparents immigrated to America from Italy in the early twentieth century. They arrived speaking Italian, but quickly learned English and did not teach their children Italian. They preserved other aspects of their culture - religion, food, music - but they were careful about not appearing "too Italian." They assimilated into American culture as much as an Italian family could at the time.

As a result, none of their children speak Italian and other aspects of the culture were lost. Growing up, I honestly never "felt Italian," even though I had an Italian last name. Years later, my grandmother took me to Italy to teach me about her childhood, and I understood our family's Italian story.

Indian immigrants have shared with me their concerns about their American children losing their Indian culture. The pressure on my Italian family to assimilate years ago are not as strong today, but it does take effort to build a sense of cultural identity when your culture is not the dominant one.

What is the "salad bowl"?

The salad bowl is the melting pot without the heat. Ethnic identities aren't melted and reformed, but co-exist.

Immigrants in the 1970's and after arrived in a different America than those before them. It's not that the immigrants today are different, but America is different. Today many families want their children to know the language and culture from their home country. In our neighborhood children go to Saturday morning programs like Chinese School, Greek School and Hindi School. Passing on the culture is taken seriously and not unAmerican.

Groups that had been marginalized are now organized and demand recognition, respect and enforcement of their rights. Popular culture celebrates diversity, multiculturalism and feminism, and there is an increasing awareness of the effects of colonialism and oppression. Whereas the term Italian-American did not exist when my grandparents arrived, hyphenated names like African-American, Hispanic-American, Arab-American are now in our vocabulary. Some complain that we are too fragmented and "identity politics" is threatening our national unity.

So which one is America?

Probably a mix of both - perhaps a vegetable soup? The melting pot has cooled down, giving ethnicities the space and freedom to maintain their form. Even in a salad bowl, there is a national culture that we all assimilate into to some degree. When done right, this vegetable soup can be delicious.

Who were the Native Americans, and where are they today?

You may have heard that Columbus "discovered" America, but

that is just one of the American myths you will learn about in this book. Columbus landed in the Caribbean islands, Central and South America. He did not land in North America at all.

You may think, "North, Central, South America...what's the difference?" Sadly, there is not as much unity on the American continent as you would think. We are far from one people of the Americas. That aside, you cannot even say that Columbus "discovered" the Caribbean or Central or South America. People were living in these places when he arrived - the native people. In America, these are known as Native Americans.

Last summer my family attended the Shinnecock Indian pow wow. The pow wow is held every year on the Shinnecock reservation in Southampton, New York. As we drove east and talked about the history of Native Americans on Long Island, I realized my daughter did not know that Native Americans still exist and live among us.

"You mean we are actually going to see Native Americans?" she asked.

For many, the image of Native Americans has been set in place by the First Thanksgiving and has not evolved. My daughter assumed Native Americans were gone because she had never met one. According to the 2010 U.S. Census, Native Americans are .09% of the American population, and about half live on reservations. Native Americans don't own the land on reservations. The land is held by the federal government and managed by Native American tribes.

This history between American settlers and Native Americans is complicated and misunderstood. For example, some Americans may not realize that Native Americans pay taxes (with some exceptions for income earned on the reservation), are U.S. citizens with the right to vote and often serve in the military defending the country.

What is important to know is that Native Americans are still alive and part of American society, although their numbers are small.

· · ·

But Native American tribal names are everywhere in America.

Massachusetts, Delaware, Miami, Illinois, Iowa, Missouri, the Cleveland Indians, Washington Redskins - tribal names are used for countless American states, cities and sports teams. I would like to think this was to honor Native people and their culture, but I'm not sure.

Native Americans find some uses of tribal names offensive, and have only been partly successful in convincing Americans to change them. This has been the case with tribal names for sports teams and mascots, which to some Native Americans are insulting and misrepresent their culture as overly violent and aggressive.

Why are Native Americans called Indians?

There are several theories for this, but one of the most popular is that Columbus mistakenly believed he had reached the East Indies (South East Asia) when he landed in the Bahamas. It is not because he thought he had landed in India, even though he was looking for a route to India. This theory has been disproven because when Columbus sailed in 1492, India was known as Hindustan, not India.

So which word should I use - "Native American" or "Indian"?

Some Native Americans prefer to be called "Indian" and not "Native American" or "American Indian." This is because including "American" in their name ignores the fact that they predate the arrival of the European explorer Amerigo Vespucci, for whom "America" is named. The term "Indian" is not considered offensive to Native-Americans, which is different than "negro" or "nigger," which are highly offensive to African-Americans.

Many Native Americans ask to be identified by their particular tribe. The best practice is to observe how people identify themselves, and follow their example. In Canada, native people use the name "First Nations."

But if I call Native Americans "Indian" what do I call myself?

South Asians generally call themselves Indians, and since they outnumber Native Americans to such a significant degree, there isn't as much confusion as you might think. In formal settings, news reporting, names of organizations and academic departments, I see "South Asian" used most often. This will also be the category you'll check on tests, surveys and job applications. But in casual communication, using Indian or Indian-American for people from India is common and accepted.

Are Puerto Ricans American?

Puerto Rico was given to the U.S. by Spain at the end of the Spanish-American War (1899). Puerto Rico is a territory of the U.S. It is not a state. Puerto Ricans do not have U.S. voting rights or pay U.S. income taxes.

What does "the browning of America" mean?

I hate this term because it implies that "brown" is somehow bad. According to the U.S. Census, by 2020, whites under age eighteen will be the minority in the U.S. for the first time. Some think this fear is driving the anti-immigration movement in the country. I'm not sure if that is true, but the "browning of America" is used by certain politicians to motivate white voters.

My mixed-race children have never heard this term, but I am prepared for the day that they do. I have armed them with an understanding that skin color does not determine what kind of person you are. I make a point to teach them about the strength, resilience and achievements of brown people to counter what they might hear in the outside world. I also teach them that ignorance is often the result of fear, insecurity and jealousy, and they shouldn't give it any power over them.

If all Americans except Native Americans are immigrants, why aren't Americans more accepting of immigrants?

As a white person, I hear other whites complain that neighborhoods are "all Asian now," or that you walk the streets of Manhattan and don't even hear English. Indian immigrants interviewed for this book have had Americans yell, "Go back to your country." This is not the majority, but I'm including it for an important reason.

I want you to understand that these comments have nothing to do with you. These speakers are repeating a familiar cycle in American history and don't even realize it. A backlash against immigrants is as American as apple pie. Some European immigrants may have forgotten how unwelcome they felt when they came to America. One of our most famous and beloved founding fathers, Benjamin Franklin, warned of the danger that German immigrants would outnumber British Americans and put the English language at risk.

You will find that Americans in general are welcoming and interested in other cultures. The vast majority know that we are all in this together.

5

BECOMING AN AMERICAN - THE IMMIGRATION SYSTEM

S ay the word "visa" to most Americans and they will think you are talking about a credit card. If Americans want to travel abroad, all they need is a passport and money. A passport is easy to get and rarely denied. There is no trip to the consulate to ask for permission to leave the country. I have seen how arbitrary the Indian consulate can be in its decisions on who can and can't get a visa. Americans would be shocked to learn Indians need to prove they have a reason to leave the country - work, school, a family event like a wedding. Americans don't have to explain their reason for travel to anyone. They just go.

Many Americans do not understand that their immigration system is incredibly slow and complicated. They might be surprised to learn that there are per country limits on the number of green cards given each year, so where you come from impacts how long you wait. According to the State Department, some American citizens of Mexican and Filipino ancestry are still waiting on applications to sponsor family members that were filed in the 1990's.

. . .

Who are the Indian immigrants?

The Asian American population has grown 72% from 2000 to 2015, which is the fastest of any other group.[1] As of 2015, 20% of Asian Americans were Indian, compared to 24% Chinese. Indian immigrants have the highest median income of Asian Americans, roughly $100,000. You are arriving on a tide of Asian American immigration. No, it's more like a tidal wave.

What is the per country limit?

No country's share of employment and family based green cards can exceed 7% of the total granted by the U.S. government per year. This is known as the per country limit, and it is the main reason for citizenship delays for immigrants from countries with a high volume of immigrants. In 2017, the limit for any one country was 25,620 (7% of the green cards granted for employment and family sponsorship).

How long is the current wait for Indians to get a green card?

The current average wait for Indian immigrants is nine to twelve years. Indians face the longest delay for employment based citizenship. For family based citizenship, Indians experience the third longest delay, behind Mexico and the Philippines.

Why is it called a "Green Card"?

The card was initially green, then changed to peach in 1989 and back to green in 2010. These cards are heavily counterfeited, so the government applies holograms and embedded data to genuine cards.

What is the status of the H1-B program?

As you likely know, the H1-B program provides 85,000 visas

each year for highly skilled workers, with 20,000 of these visas reserved for immigrants with a Master's degree or higher. These caps are met within days after the H1-B application period opens.

About 80% of H1-B visas go to Indians. This high number has led people to question whether Indian outsourcing firms and U.S. companies are manipulating the system to get visas for what are actually entry level, low wage labor. President Trump has ordered greater scrutiny of H1-B applications, limiting H1-B visas for the most highly skilled and highest paid positions, and restricting the right of H1-B spouses to work in the U.S.

What is "H-1B jail"?

This term refers to the delay in processing green cards for workers on H1-B visas. Workers are forced to stay with their sponsoring employer until their visa converts to a green card. As a result, talented Indian immigrants are stuck - they cannot leave their job for a better position or start their own company. Business leaders have realized this harms the U.S. economy, and causes Indian immigrants to settle in other countries.[2]

This has become such a problem that Congress proposed the Fairness for High Skilled Immigrants Act to fix it.

What is the Fairness for High Skilled Immigrants Act?

This Act was first introduced in 2017, but the Republican majority in the House of Representatives did not allow it out of committee (meaning there was no vote).

In 2018, Democrats became the majority party in the House of Representatives and introduced the Fairness for High Skilled Immigrants Act of 2019. The Senate introduced a similar law. Both the Senate and House draft laws were introduced by a Republican and Democrat, which is promising. California Senator Kamala Harris, who is of Indian and African American ancestry, introduced the bill in the Senate.

The 2019 proposal eliminates the per country limits for employment based immigration. The total number of green cards issued each year does not change, and the cap on overall employment based immigration remains. Family based immigration would still have a per country cap, but this would increase from 7% to 15% of the total.

How does a person become an American citizen?

These are the ways to become an American citizen:

1. Born on American soil (even if your parents are not citizens).
2. Born to U.S. citizens, or at least one parent who is a U.S. citizen, anywhere in the world.
3. The "naturalization process" - This is a very strange name for a citizenship process. It sounds more like a cleansing or forced time in nature. "Naturalization" is a ten step process that begins with a visa, leads to a Permanent Resident Card ("Green Card") and then after years of waiting, full citizenship. The most common way to begin the process is with a student, work or family sponsorship visa. You must be at least eighteen years old, able to read, write and speak basic English, be of good moral character, sit for a test and interview, show continuous residence in the U.S. and take an oath of allegiance to the U.S.A.
4. Diversity Visa Program (Green Card lottery) - The diversity lottery favors countries with low numbers of immigrants. Since so many Indians apply, there is a cap on the number of Indians selected through the lottery. It runs two years behind and you have to register to be eligible. The lottery is usually held in the fall. This has been criticized by the Trump administration, even though it is incredibly rare for an Indian to "win" this lottery.
5. Millionaire visa - This is just what it sounds like - the

green card is awarded to someone who invests one million dollars in a U.S. business that creates or preserves at least ten permanent full-time jobs for U.S. workers.

6. Asylum - Asylum is based on the international law that no country can return people to their home country if they are fleeing persecution. This humanitarian law was first adopted by the UN Commission on Refugees and then by the U.S. Over the past few years, the vast majority of asylum seekers in the U.S. have been from Central America. Asylum seekers must pass an initial screening to assess the threat facing them in their home country. If they pass this screening at the border, they can legally stay in America until the date of their court hearing. For various reasons, less than half of those who pass the screening show up at the hearing. The Trump administration alleges that asylum seekers use persecution as an excuse to gain entry into the country. However, the Trump administration cannot abandon its obligation to international law on asylum. Instead, it has slowed the processing of these claims, separated families at the border and placed asylum seekers in detention. Indians seeking asylum are usually Sikhs and Christians claiming religious persecution.

7. Temporary Protected Status (TPS) visa- The TPS visa can be applied for when an immigrant is already in America, as long as the immigrant is in the country legally. It is for people from countries where conditions make it impossible for them to return, at least in the short term. For example, Nepalis in the U.S. were eligible for TPS after the devastating 2015 earthquake. The Trump administration has been bringing many of these TPS programs to a close. India is not on the TPS list.

8. T Visa - The T visa is available for victims of human trafficking who cooperate with law enforcement. Human trafficking includes sex trafficking and labor trafficking, and has become a wide-ranging global problem,

particularly in India, Nepal and Bangladesh. Victims are often afraid to turn on their trafficker and do not trust American authorities. This visa is a way to protect and earn the trust of victims who help bring the trafficker to justice.

What if I fail the naturalization (citizenship) test?

You can retake the part that you failed.

What is an illegal (also called undocumented) immigrant?

The term "illegal" immigrant refers to an immigrant living in the U.S. that is not a legal citizen or in the process of becoming a legal citizen (for example, through one of the ways described above). They are also called illegal aliens, out of status, or undocumented immigrants.

If you are an illegal immigrant in America, there is currently no way to become legal. There have been proposals to change this - for example, allowing immigrants to apply for a green card if they voluntarily come forward, pay a fine and have a clean criminal record - but these proposals have been rejected. Critics say it is unfair to grant "amnesty" to those who broke the law, and this will only encourage more immigrants to enter illegally. This type of amnesty has been granted before, though, even by Republican presidents (in 1986 Republican President Ronald Reagan gave amnesty to 3 million illegal immigrants).

Why are there so many illegal immigrants in America?

The dirty secret is that most American citizens and American businesses benefit from the cheap labor provided by illegal immigrants. There is a market for this labor, and always will be. You will hear talk about the dangers of open borders, but from what I have seen in corporate America, the borders are open for a reason.

Corporations profit from open borders. Even President Trump's private businesses have been caught hiring undocumented workers.

The other dirty secret is that since 2000, when 1.6 million illegal immigrants were stopped at the border, the number of crossings is now closer to 400,000. That is a drop by three quarters. Whereas most immigrants at the border in 2000 were from Mexico, the highest numbers now are from the Central American countries of Guatemala, Honduras and El Salvador. These countries suffer from extreme poverty, corruption and violence.

As of 2014, there were approximately 12 million illegal immigrants in the U.S. For obvious reasons it is difficult to determine the real number, but if we use the 12 million estimate, then illegal immigrants constitute about 3.5% of the U.S. population.

Are there many Indian illegal immigrants?

You may be surprised to learn that as of 2014, Indians were the fourth largest illegal immigrant population in America, behind Mexico, El Salvador and Guatemala. Asian-Americans are 13% of the undocumented immigrants. Of this 13%, India tops the list, followed by China, the Philippines and Korea.

How do Indians become illegal?

Most Indians become illegal by overstaying a visa. They do not cross the U.S./Mexican border, so you will not hear much about them on the news or from politicians. However, government action against visa fraud and overstaying visas is increasing. As I discuss in the chapter on Education (College), the government recently raided a fake school used by Indians to extend their visas (known as a "visa mill"). Some police are checking visa status on simple stops like speeding or other traffic violations.

What are the risks of overstaying a visa?

Overstaying a visitor visa without obtaining an extension is not a wise way to stay in the country. You will not be on a path to citizenship, you could be sent to a horrific detention center, and when deported you could wait up to ten years to return, if you are allowed to return at all.

What can illegal immigrants do and not do?

Illegal immigrants can't get a Social Security Number, but they can apply to the Internal Revenue Service (IRS) for an Individual Taxpayer Identification Number (ITIN). The IRS does not check citizenship status before assigning an ITIN. This number can then be used to obtain work, open a bank account, pay taxes, and get a driver's license in some states.

Why hasn't President Trump attacked the use of ITINs by illegal immigrants? Simply put - money earned by ITIN holders is taxed, which brings billions of dollars to the government every year.

Children of illegal immigrants can attend school in the U.S. Many of these children and their parents receive health benefits through state programs, and cannot be turned away from the hospital if they need emergency care. They can buy homes with cash or seek an ITIN mortgage, which is not common but does exist.

It is very risky for illegal immigrants to leave the country, and even riskier for them to try to get back in. But as you can see, for a country with a leader opposed to illegal immigration, undocumented workers in the U.S. can have a comfortable life.

Whom can I sponsor?

President Trump has called for an end to "chain migration" - the term he uses for citizens and permanent residents sponsoring family members. Of course, his criticism ignores the fact that his immigrant wife applied to sponsor her European parents for citizenship.

Overall approvals of sponsorship applications have dropped by a quarter during the Tump administration. Delays have grown longer, and the government says it is prioritizing other applications.

The new Democratic Congress has responded with action to protect family based immigration. The Fairness for High Skilled Immigrants Act of 2019 (discussed above) attempts to increase the per country limit on family based immigration from 7% to 15%, which would be a positive for Indian immigrants.

Is the Trump trying to reduce legal immigration to the U.S.?

The Trump administration supports the RAISE Act, which would cut by half the number of immigrants granted permanent resident status over the next ten years (from the current one million per year to five hundred thousand per year). The Act would accomplish this by eliminating categories of family sponsorship and adopting a points system for employment based sponsorship. Family sponsorship would only be allowed for spouses and minor children of U.S. citizens. This extreme measure will never pass in Congress, and is not supported by mainstream Republicans.

Many of Trump's positions on immigration, such as the border wall and eliminating family based sponsorship, are not shared by the majority of Americans. These radical proposals were on the fringes before he was elected. Now those fringe groups have access to the White House and are influencing the President, who repeats them loudly and without factual support. Fortunately, in America, it is Congress and not the President that makes the law of the land.

What is the status of the border wall?

Where is that "big, beautiful wall" President Trump promised during the campaign? President Trump signed an executive order for the 2,000 mile border wall, but he needs Congress to pay for it. That has been the problem. The 2018 mid-term election shifted majority power in the House of Representatives to Democrats, who are opposed to the border wall. The refusal of Democrats to give the President the billions he requested for the wall led to a government shut-down in early 2019, and Congress denying the president his funds. President Trump responded by declaring that illegal border crossings are a "National Emergency" that requires him to pull money from other government agencies to build the wall. More than fifteen lawsuits were filed to challenge this declaration. This issue will be debated in the courts for years.

Can I serve in the military before I am a citizen?

Yes, but you must be a legal resident. An undocumented immigrant cannot serve in the military.

Do I have to pay taxes if I am not yet a citizen? Why?

Most likely. You should pay taxes because it documents your intention to stay and build a life in America. You can pay taxes with an ITIN number. Many illegal immigrants also pay taxes to establish a credit record. This is discussed in greater detail in the Taxes chapter.

Is dual citizenship allowed in America?

Yes.

6

THE AMERICAN WORKPLACE

An Indian immigrant told me a story about her first Friday afternoon at work in America. She did not understand why her co-workers told her to, "Have a nice weekend!" She thought to herself, "What is so special about the weekend?"

She soon realized that Americans work so much during the week that the weekend is the only time for rest and enjoyment.

Another Indian immigrant said she feels more comfortable in the workplace than in social situations because at work she is valued for her skills. This immigrant grew up in a rural Indian village and had a heavy accent when she arrived here. She was nervous to speak, but confident at work because she was on familiar ground, practicing her skill. Deadlines, teamwork and problem solving were more important than her Indian accent or cultural misunderstandings.

What if my employer is sponsoring me for a work visa?

Immigrants sponsored by employers must keep in mind that if they quit, they lose their legal status in the U.S. This is also the case if you get fired, unless you find another employer to sponsor you.

Employers are legally required to inform the government that you are no longer working with the sponsoring company.

You are still protected by American employment law even if you are not a citizen of this country. Still, every immigrant I spoke with told me that until they had a green card, they did not risk their employment based sponsorship by speaking up about their salary, work assignments or treatment by managers or co-workers.

Will my co-workers know my visa status?

Only if you tell them. Discrimination based on immigration status is illegal in the U.S. This means legal immigrants can't be treated differently than non-immigrants because of their immigration status. A potential employer cannot ask job applicants their citizenship status. All an employer can do is inform applicants that if they get the job they will have to prove that they are lawfully permitted to work in the U.S.

Do workers know the salaries of their co-workers?

Usually not, but this depends on the company and industry. For example, law firms have a step-by-step salary structure for associates based on years of experience. All first year associates are paid the same rate, except for the end of the year bonus, which is based on hours billed. In most industries, pay is not as clear, fair or transparent.

Salaries of executives at public companies are also made public in annual filings with the Securities and Exchange Commission. These salaries do not include bonus income, which does not have to be disclosed.

In general, employee salaries are carefully guarded by the Human Resources Department. Employers feel that revealing salary information is a distraction that divides workers and creates a competitive, negative work environment. This may be true, but others claim that such secrecy allows for favoritism and wage discrimination.

. . .

What should I know about getting a job in America?

An Indian information technology (IT) professional working in Manhattan told me she feels that in the U.S. "networking is everything." She doesn't mean wireless networks. She was referring to building relationships at work that can help you find your next job. This immigrant started under one manager and has followed him and his group to several different companies. Except for her first job, every other job was at a company where she knew someone already working there. Her network is more than professional - they trust each other and watch out for each other. These colleagues even come to birthday parties for her children. She is the only Indian in the group.

To get a first job in America, it helps to have something non-Indian on your resume. Some immigrants who come for marriage, for example, take courses here or volunteer to get experience. The IT professional mentioned above worked for a major consulting firm in India and handled American clients, but she was still nervous that American employers would not value her Indian work experience as much as work done in America.

While studying for certification exams immigrants often work jobs on the side. One immigrant told me he worked fourteen hours a day and was paid $5 an hour packing sodas into a store cooler section. He was amazed how many brands and flavors of soda exist in America. He was paid below the state mandated "minimum wage" ($12 in New York as of December 31, 2018) and a fourteen hour day violates labor laws, but he was grateful for the work.

How should I interact with my manager?

According to one Indian immigrant, in India you work "under" a manager, but in the U.S. you work "with" your manager. There is a team feeling, and managers care more about your well being. Managers want work to be completed, but understand that a stressful and competitive work environment may not be the best way to accomplish this.

Indian formalities such as standing when a manager enters the room and refraining from eating in front of a manager may seem awkward in America and are not expected. There is a greater sense of equality between employees and managers. One immigrant was surprised that her manager said hello and talked to workers at all levels in the company.

How do you "move up" at work?

In America it does not matter where you come from, only where you want to go and how hard you are willing to work for it. But how do you work for it? How do you "move up the ladder" at work?

In India, bribery, corruption and prejudice can be obstacles to career advancement. Connections and influence matter more than merit. This was the case with my father-in-law, and many of our relatives. Family members who came to America are thankful that here they are judged by how hard they work.

But to succeed in the American workplace, you have to do more than work long hours. You have to work smart. Work product matters, so don't make mistakes. If you do make mistakes, learn from them. More importantly, be a team player. Teamwork is very important in American companies. Be a creative thinker - companies are always looking for innovative and outside the box solutions. Pursuing higher education and training shows curiosity and dedication. Flexibility is critical, especially in today's evolving marketplace. My husband started in IT and when those jobs were outsourced, he changed careers.

Loyalty is not as important as it used to be. American workers change jobs frequently. This is partly due to layoffs, but also because the only opportunity to move up and earn more may be at a different company.

Corporate managers complain that workers should be more loyal, especially millennials (born after the year 2000). Young workers are often viewed as selfish and impatient. They want to run their own company rather than work for someone else. They think they know everything, despite their youth. These are not traits preferred by today's employers.

Of course, there will always be other factors in your success at work, and some are beyond your control. Your company is downsizing, or is trying to promote more women and you are a man. Do what is expected of you, and do it well. A law school professor once told me you'd be amazed how many people don't follow that simple advice.

Can I ask for a raise?

Yes. One Indian immigrant told me this was very different than in India, where employees wait for a raise instead of asking for one. Indians assume their hard work will be noticed and rewarded. This is not the case for most Americans. It is common for American employees to ask for a raise, and even threaten to leave if they don't get one.

Can I really be fired for something I say at work?

Yes - so be careful. Freedom of speech does not apply to the workplace. In the office, your employer makes the rules about what speech is acceptable and what speech has a negative impact on work. These rules don't just apply to words you speak - be careful in your emails, social media posts, memos and even gestures.

This is an area where someone unfamiliar with the culture can get into trouble. Be cautious. If there is a chance your speech could offend others, don't speak. It simply is not worth the risk of ruining your career over a misunderstanding.

What is sexual harassment?

There are two types of sexual harassment under U.S. law. The first is a Latin phrase - *quid pro quo* - which means "this for that." In *quid pro quo* sexual harassment, one person demands sex or something of a sexual nature from another person in exchange for a work benefit (for example, a raise or promotion).

I remember sitting in a sexual harassment training at work and being told that *quid pro quo* sexual harassment doesn't happen anymore. I raised my hand and said, "It used to happen a lot, and that's why we have these laws." What the #metoo movement taught us is that *quid pro quo* sexual harassment still does happen.

The second type of sexual harassment defined by law is called "hostile work environment." This is when one person behaves in such an offensive manner that it creates a hostile work environment for the person being harassed. A violation can happen once (if it is very severe), or be a pattern of continuous activity. It doesn't have to be actions, either - gestures, displaying certain types of materials in the workplace, writing or forwarding emails - these all count as harassment. The action is viewed from the point of view of the person receiving the harassment, so "I didn't know she was offended," isn't an excuse.

An employee cannot be fired for reporting sexual harassment. Many states now mandate sexual harassment training, so if you are told to attend one of these meetings don't think you are being singled out.

Why do Americans need to "love" their jobs?

A first generation Indian interning as a data scientist for an insurance company told me, "The work is interesting and I am learning a lot, but…I just don't care about it." A generation before, you would not hear talk about "caring for" or "loving" your work, especially from an immigrant. But this intern, born and raised in America, had the luxury of finding a job that she cared about.

A Indian doctor told me the reason so many Indians are doctors is because it is a secure job. "No matter what happens," she said, "people always need doctors." When you come from a poor country, she explained, security is everything. In a rich country like America, self fulfillment and happiness can seem more important than security.

The good news is that you can find a job with meaning in America, if that is what you want. Today, more companies strive to be socially responsible. There is an acceptance that "doing good" can be good for business. With the help of social media, companies build communities and mobilize them to do good. The rise of these types of companies in the U.S. makes it easier to find a job with meaning beyond your paycheck.

Is there a backlash against Indian professionals?

I have spoken to Indians who feel the backlash is real. They point to the Trump administration immigration policies and the popular perception that Indians are "stealing jobs" from Americans. Others say they have never been treated differently in America based on their Indian identity. Some choose not to focus on any backlash and instead see excelling at work as the way to silence critics.

This is how the older generation of Indian immigrants handled it. Indian doctors who came in the 1970's had their credentials questioned by fellow colleagues. Patients were sent to other doctors, and when Indian doctors did see patients they had to defend their conclusions. These professionals persevered and are now highly respected.

How should I handle the backlash?

As a white person in America, it isn't appropriate for me to answer this question. All I can say is what I would tell my children.

My children are too young to be in the workplace, but not too young to overhear comments about "too many Indians." I believe the root cause of this is fear and misinformation. Some fear what is theirs will be taken away, that they are being left behind, or that what they knew and loved is changing too quickly. Do not let this fear change how you view yourself or your right to be here. Look to the example of those who came before you, and do not give in to those unable to appreciate all you have to offer.

. . .

The workplace appears much more social in America than in India.

Americans spend a lot of time at work. Once I asked a partner at a law firm where to drop off a memo, and she pointed down the hall and said, "I live down there." She was speaking about her office, but she probably spent more time in her office than her real home. In the past, law firms had showers for lawyers who spent the whole night at work.

It makes sense that American co-workers become friends and share more of their lives with each other than they might in other countries. Casual chatting about sports, family and entertainment is common (known as "water cooler" talk for the days when workers gathered around the shared water cooler). Colleagues meet for lunch and after work cocktails (called "happy hour"). Politics, once a popular topic of conversation, has been banned from some offices because it can threaten a productive work environment.

Young, hip technology companies eager to hire in demand talent promote a fun, relaxed atmosphere at work. These sprawling office "campuses" offer table tennis, exercise classes, cafeterias and other perks. Be careful, though - the companies with laundry, shower and eating facilities on site often do so because their workers have no free time away from the office.

What about drinking at work events?

This is where most employees get into trouble. Sadly, employees give in to the temptation of free drinks. Overstressed workers may be thankful for the chance to relax. What starts as a social break can destroy relationships and careers.

Never, ever get drunk at work events - this includes business trips, company outings, office parties, even business lunches or dinners. You may see your co-workers, male or female, and even your boss, drinking to excess. Everyone laughs and you may not think there are any consequences. The truth is people laugh because they do not know what else to do. As for consequences - they exist. It might be a warning or a note in your employment file. Worse than that, your reputation will be ruined, no matter how excellent your work.

What are all of these forms I am signing on my first day?

There is a lot of paperwork in America. Work is no exception. On your first day of work, you will be presented with stacks of forms to read and sign. Don't worry, it isn't a test. Take your time and look through the papers.

To help you, below is an explanation of the common forms given to new employees:

W-4

Tax worksheet used to indicate how many deductions you want withheld from your paycheck. Don't confuse it with a W-2, which is the document you receive from your employer at the end of the year reporting your annual income and taxes withheld at work. The W-4 is not sent to the government, just held by the employer.

I-9

Your employer uses the I-9 to verify your employment eligibility. You will need to show two forms of photo identification. This is not sent to the government.

Health/vision/dental insurance forms

These benefits may not start on the first day. You have to wait for the "open enrollment" period. Some jobs also make you wait a specified period before getting benefits.

Employment Agreement

This is not required for all employees. It is usually for executive level employees.

Employee Manual

These rules of the workplace are very important- you can be terminated for violating them. Most rights can be restricted in the workplace if they interfere with work performance.

Non-compete/Non-Solicitation Clauses

These legal clauses restrict what you do after you leave the company, and often prevent you from working for a competitor for a set period of time or soliciting former coworkers to join you at your new job. They are found in an Employment Agreement or Employee Manual.

Intellectual Property Assignment

This document asks you to list any intellectual property you currently own. Whatever you include on the list belongs to you and not your employer. Anything you create during your employment - even outside of work hours if you are using work materials or equipment - may be considered a "work-made-for-hire" and legally owned by your employer.

Social Media Policy

This policy explains when and what kind of social media use is permitted during work hours. Employees are representatives of the company, and can be fired for social media posts, even posts made outside of work hours.

What is an at-will employee?

An at-will employee can be fired at any time, for any reason or for no reason at all (known as "without cause") - as long as the termination does not violate federal or state anti-discrimination laws. An H1-B worker, and most workers in the U.S., are considered at-will.

What is a union?

You may hear the terms "organized labor" or "union." These are membership organizations for workers that negotiate with management for benefits such as health insurance, pensions and holiday time. Members pay dues, and often there is little choice whether or not to join. Unions are found in schools, factories, warehouses, trade workers like electricians, police and firefighters. It is extremely rare to find unions in the technology sector or for high skilled jobs.

Unions say they protect workers, but management responds that they drive up the price of labor. In the case of manufacturing, union labor is cited as one of the reasons companies move overseas.

What is the E.E.O.C. and workplace discrimination?

It is quite easy for American workers to file a discrimination claim against an employer. The E.E.O.C. is the Equal Employment Opportunity Commission, the federal administrative body that receives and reviews employment discrimination complaints. You do not need a lawyer to file an E.E.O.C. complaint, and the form is short and basic. Employees can also sue in federal or state court, but filing with the E.E.O.C. is much cheaper, quicker and easier.

U.S. law protects individuals from workplace discrimination based on the following characteristics: race, color, gender, religion, national origin, age (40 and over) and genetic status (for example, having a genetic disease). Companies are not allowed to retaliate against employees who file E.E.O.C. complaints. Revoking an employment visa or deporting an illegal immigrant are unlawful forms of retaliation.

What is the best state for employees? For business owners?

Employment is largely governed by state law. Some states favor the rights of workers (California), others favor business owners (Texas). Factors to consider when comparing states as an employee are: state taxes, leave policies, worker protections, the minimum wage and cost of living.

Why is so much money taken out of my paycheck?

Receiving your first paycheck in America is like opening a present only to find half of it missing. Below is an explanation of what is taken out.

Federal and State Income Tax Deductions

This amount is based on how much you chose to deduct on your W-4. If you end up deducting more than you owe at the end of the year, you will receive a refund when you pay your taxes. During tax time you will hear a lot of talk about "refunds" and "money back."

Medicare and Social Security Tax Deductions

These are referred to as the F.I.C.A. taxes (Federal Insurance Contributions Act). The idea is you are paying for the Medicare and Social Security that you will eventually receive when you are a senior citizen.

Health/vision/dental Insurance Premiums

Even though your employer is providing health insurance, you still have to pay the monthly premium. This may seem high, but it is significantly less than what you would pay to buy insurance on the open market. Most people in the U.S. get their health insurance through their employer.

Net "take home" pay

Finally! This is the amount that goes into your pocket or bank account.

Are American companies required to offer paid maternity/paternity leave?

No. Under the Family Medical Leave Act (FMLA), employees at companies with more than fifty employees can take up to twelve weeks of unpaid leave to care for a newborn or adopted child. Unlike many other wealthy nations, America does not have a federal law mandating paid maternity/paternity leave. Some states and cities have better paid leave laws, and companies can always offer additional benefits to their employees.

What is meant by the term "gig economy"?

This refers to short-term, freelance, project-based work (a gig). These gigs don't come with benefits or promises of future work. They give the worker freedom to find work with multiple employers, and thanks to the internet, sometimes all over the world.

. . .

What does "off the books" mean?

If you are paid in cash, there is a strong chance you are being paid "off the books." This means that both parties to the transaction are not reporting the income to the government. So the person paying you is not paying payroll and other required taxes, and you are not paying tax on the money earned. There are risks. If caught, you will have to pay a fine and your visa could be in jeopardy. You could be caught if the person who paid you is caught. The government will come after you looking for its tax money.

But how do some Americans get free government services without working?

The U.S. government provides health insurance for free to low income citizens who qualify. This is called Medicaid. Low income people also receive housing subsidies (Section 8) from the federal government, and many states provide free health care for children living in poverty.

This may sound like socialism, and it is. America is not a pure market economy. There is a "safety net" - government services intended to help those who need it either for a short period (unemployment benefits) or permanently (disability benefits). Tax dollars fund these benefits, and for that reason the cost of government benefits is always a hot political issue.

Whenever a free benefit is offered, there is going to be corruption and dishonesty. These benefits can have the effect of discouraging work if money earned would be less than the amount received in benefits. One of the immigrants I interviewed is a doctor for the low income population. He commented that there is nothing like these benefits in India. "If you are poor and sick in India," he said, "you die."

7

WOMEN AT WORK

I 'll never forget a conversation I had at work with an Indian colleague about fifteen years my senior. Our favorite manager had just left the company after years of excellent work that was undervalued. Her departure made me start thinking I would leave soon as well. My colleague and I both knew it was a difficult place for women to work.

"Still," she said in her cheerful manner, "I love my job."

She must have seen the surprise on my face.

"You see," she went on, "I came to this country a bride of nineteen years old. I spoke no English. So for me, to have this position… I am just so proud."

I was proud of her, too. Suddenly our complaints seemed trivial compared to what she overcame to sit where she was today - behind a big wooden desk, in her own office, a financial professional at a large American company.

When I decided to write this book, she was my first interview. You will find some of her advice below.

Are women treated equally at work?

This is a difficult question to answer, since it depends on the industry, position and personalities on your team. Traditionally, male dominated industries are more difficult for women. This isn't always intentional - if management is not familiar with the needs of women, they can't be sensitive to them. This presents an opportunity to educate management, if they are open to learning.

The main issues for women in the workplace are equal pay for equal work (referred to as the "gender pay gap"), sexual harassment and flexible work arrangements (working from home, part-time schedules). Companies led by women tend to have more favorable policies for women. Powerful women's groups have also been successful advocates for change in certain industries. For example, female venture capitalists have come together to mentor and invest in female founders. It is this type of support that will empower women to create better work environments for all employees.

What is the work culture like for women in the technology industry?

Female engineers are a minority in technology companies. Some of these engineers say the tech culture leaves them feeling like they don't belong. The culture for women in the tech industry became a national discussion in the summer of 2017, when a Google engineer criticized the company's efforts to hire more female engineers. The engineer was fired. In response, the engineer claimed Google wasn't an open culture and he was punished for speaking the truth.

The debate that followed focused on how to increase female representation in technology companies and whether this is a valid goal in the first place. If men are better suited for engineering work, argued the engineer, then hiring more female engineers is actually bad for the company. The "science" the engineer relied on to claim men are superior engineers was highly disputed. The engineer had also ignored the role of society in steering women away from engineering, a problem many tech companies are trying to correct through investments in education.

One of the challenges is that schools aren't graduating enough female engineers to meet the demand. According to some, this leads companies to hire under qualified women for the sake of gender parity. Should a company like Google, which not only builds the products shaping the future but also must answer to shareholders, place gender parity above hiring the best candidate? At the same time, isn't it better for all of us if a diverse team is building products for a diverse world?

What are my rights to equal pay for equal work?

An employer cannot pay a male and female different amounts for the same work, unless there is a reason unrelated to gender why the pay rates are different.

Still, the reported pay rate for women is about 80-82 cents for every dollar a male makes. This data is controversial and economists cite other reasons for the pay gap unrelated to gender.

What should I look for in selecting an employer?

There are signs to look for in picking a company that supports women. First, consider how many women are in management and how long they have been there. If women come and go, that could be a sign they are not valued. Second, investigate the company maternity leave policy. A company with paid maternity leave longer than three months is usually supportive of women on other issues, too. Third, what work flexibility arrangements do they offer, and more importantly, are women who take advantage of these options penalized in assignments or advancement?

Many companies say they are flexible, but the reality is different when you are on the job. You may not want to raise this in an interview, but speak with some female employees and they will give you the truth.

What if I want to take time away from work to raise my children. Can I return to work after?

Women who have the most success returning to the workplace after a few years away are those who remain involved in the field. Keep in touch with co-workers, maintain your certifications/licenses and perhaps improve your skills if you can do so online or when time allows. To keep your skills sharp, consider contract or part-time work. This shows a dedication to the profession over the long term. Without evidence of your continued growth and involvement as a professional, it is harder to convince an employer to hire you after a long break.

Don't expect flexibility or work-life balance the first day you are back, or the first month or year. There is a common belief with management that you have to "pay your dues" - this means show your dedication to quality work, produce quality work consistently, and then you can ask for more flexibility in your work hours.

What is the #metoo movement?

The phrase "Me Too" has been used since 2006 by the activist Tarana Burke, a sexual assault survivor. Today, the phrase is associated with the sexual assault survivor stories posted on Twitter using the hashtag #metoo. This hashtag went viral in the fall of 2017 as the accusations against prominent leaders mounted.

The movement is remarkable in the number incidents it has revealed. Many Americans were unaware that sexual assault, harassment and discrimination was such a pervasive problem in society. In the past, female victims were often criticized and doubted. While you still hear this backlash, diligent reporting and media coverage have given these accusations credibility. The public has watched, sometimes with disbelief, as men from the top ranks of every field are terminated in disgrace. Men are now facing consequences for their actions. I want to believe that the excuse "boys will be boys" is no longer accepted.

In the fall of 2018, it seemed like every week brought new accusations against respected, esteemed male professionals. This came to a high point with the nomination of Brett M. Kavanaugh to the Supreme Court, and testimony by his accuser, Christine Blasey

Ford. Even though Dr. Ford's testimony did not block Justice Kavanaugh's appointment to the Supreme Court, it sent a message to the world that is empowering victims to share their stories. I have read that this message has reached India, which is now experiencing its own #metoo movement.

Despite what you might hear from President Trump, there is not much sympathy in the U.S. for the accused men. Mainstream society does not see these men as victims. I am only telling you this because an honest, innocent question like "What about the poor men who lose everything?" could be misunderstood and have negative consequences for you.

What is feminism? Why would a woman say she is not a feminist?

Feminism is widely known as the belief that men and women should be treated equally. In America, it's more complicated, and not for the better.

Women are divided in America, just like the country. Some women feel feminists are anti-male, anti-family and anti-traditional values. Feminism is viewed as benefitting white, upper class women over the needs of working class women of color. The feminist movement has been blamed for the high rates of divorce, the breakdown of the nuclear family structure and the protection of abortion rights.

The election of Donald Trump over Hillary Clinton was seen by some feminists as evidence that the country is not ready to accept women in power. While there are women in high positions of power in the U.S., Ms. Clinton was the first woman to run for president as a Democrat or Republican.

The 2016 election and Trump's public comments and actions towards women have revived the feminist movement in America. Still, some American women prefer not to be called "feminists" even though they support equality for women.

· · ·

How important is a mentor?

It is helpful to have a group of friends at work you can trust - friends you can ask the types of questions in this book. The lady I introduced you to above said mentors were incredibly important to her career. Friends and mentors helped her overcome insecurities about her accent, and offered tips about surviving social situations like office parties.

This was echoed by other Indian women I interviewed. The camaraderie they shared with co-workers not only made work enjoyable but helped them advance in their careers.

You don't have to be an immigrant to know the role a mentor can play in your career. Mentorship programs are common, and senior employees are often flattered if a junior colleague asks them to be a mentor. Some companies arrange these pairs, others let them happen naturally through friendship, common interests or shared work goals. If you don't find a suitable mentor, ask your manager for suggestions. This will show initiative and a willingness to learn, both positives traits in the American workplace.

How do women from different generations work together in the workplace?

Most women who entered the workforce in the 1960's and 1970's were forced to make sacrifices for their career. When they started, there were no part-time or work from home options. There were no breast-pumping rooms in the workplace (yes, these do exist!). They had to overcome stereotypes that cast women as weak, emotional and less intelligent.

The conflict arises when older women expect younger women to make the same sacrifices. Younger women are labeled spoiled and unappreciative of the opportunities created by past generations. When I started as a lawyer, the only female law partners I saw were unmarried and without children. They worked long hours and received high praise from the firm. If that was "success" in the legal field, I didn't want it.

As more women set the rules and mold the workplace to the

realities of life, these conflicts are fading away. Choosing an alternate path used to be considered ungrateful, but I see it as freedom.

I know work is social, but I don't feel comfortable socializing with men at work.

The social aspect of the workplace isn't just about fun - it is also about career advancement. I remember being told as a young girl, "Learn golf because it will be good for your career." Powerful men played golf and used the time on the course for business talk. The message to girls was that if you didn't play with the boys, you would be left out of business opportunities.

I don't think playing golf is very important today, but going to lunch is. It is common for women to eat lunch with men. If a man asks you to lunch and there is a professional reason for him to do so (for example, you are working on the same project or meeting a new client), then go. If it isn't professional, don't waste your time if he asks again.

8

THE AMERICAN MEDICAL SYSTEM

Health care in America is about a lot more than life and death. It's big business, a debated political issue and the number one cause of bankruptcy for Americans. So don't think this chapter is just for Indian immigrant doctors - it's for everyone.

How do Americans get health insurance?

As of 2017, the vast majority of Americans (about 150 million) got health insurance from their employer. Sixty million received health benefits through the low income government program Medicaid, and forty million were insured by the senior citizen government program Medicare. About six million received military and veteran insurance, also provided by the government, and approximately thirty to forty million Americans were uninsured.

What is this I hear about health care being "a right" in America?

Some argue that health care is a basic human right that should be provided by the government. A healthy, educated population is good for society, even if the costs are high. There are many aspects of American policy that value the health of the individual over the cost of care. For example, federal law requires publicly funded hospital emergency rooms to treat the sick even if they cannot pay. Another example is the expansion of government subsidies for health care through "Obamacare" (the Affordable Care Act of 2010).

Does health insurance cover the full cost of treatment?

No. The part paid by patients is called a "co-pay." Co-pays are usually between $25 and $50 depending on the plan, and specialists cost more. Most offices require payment of the co-pay before you can see the doctor.

Why don't all doctors take insurance?

Doctors in private practice want to control the amount they can charge for services. They are running a business, and need to cover costs like rent, supplies, salaries and malpractice insurance. Insurance companies change the amounts they reimburse doctors, but the costs facing doctors remain the same, or increase. Doctors who do not accept insurance avoid this risk because they are paid in full by the patient, not reimbursed by insurance companies.

Doctors also may not want to manage the insurance billing process. Patients with "out of network" benefits in their insurance plans can seek reimbursement for these payments. You see non-insurance doctors in highly specialized fields and mental health services.

Is there a penalty for not having health insurance?

No. This was instituted as part of the Affordable Care Act, but was repealed in 2018.

. . .

What are some of the main issues in health care?

Other than insurance coverage, some issues that get a lot of coverage are cancer, Alzheimer's disease and abortion. There is a focus on an active lifestyle and healthy diet as preventative measures. Cancer is very common in America, and the main way to treat it is still radiation and chemotherapy, although there have been advancements in other therapies. Alzheimer's disease is on the rise in America, and there is no known cure at this time.

Abortion is not just a medical issue, but political as well. Abortion has been legal in the U.S. since 1973. The Supreme Court protected a woman's right to an abortion in the decision *Roe v. Wade*, but some states place restrictions on this right. Those against abortion are labeled "pro-life" and those for protecting a woman's right to choose are labeled "pro-choice." There is already a shortage of doctors performing abortions, and service providers such as Planned Parenthood are at risk of losing funding. It is possible that *Roe v. Wade* will be overturned, and doctors are worried about the impact this could have on at-risk pregnancies and babies needing significant medical care after birth.

Why are Americans afraid of hospitals?

"Don't go into a hospital - you may not come out." This is a popular American saying. Many people are afraid they will get an infection in a hospital, get sick from other patients or die because of some hospital error. The numbers don't support this, but the fear persists, especially among older people.

America and Mental Illness

One of the most positive developments in American health care is the open discussion of mental illness. Finally, mental illness is being treated like any other illness, without stigma or shame. Some Indian immigrants I interviewed shared that in India mental illness is still a subject that is avoided and often hidden by families.

Even with this recent recognition and acceptance of mental illness in the U.S., finding affordable treatment is still very difficult. Most mental health practitioners do not take insurance, and patients have to wait months for an initial appointment. Most practices charge over one hundred dollars a visit. For most, mental health care is just too expensive.

What is self help?

America has been called the "self help" capital of the world. Just go to the self help section of a bookstore (or Amazon) and you will understand why. The titles of books on the subject are endless, all promising a happier, more productive you. Celebrity motivational speakers such as Tony Robbins and Oprah Winfrey tell Americans they are in control of their destiny and can create the "life of their dreams." Americans love to hear this, and love to share the secrets of their success.

What is "western medicine" and "eastern medicine"?

Western medicine is the term used for the way medicine has been traditionally taught and practiced in the West. Eastern medicine emphasizes the whole body and non-pharmaceutical therapies such as yoga, acupuncture, Ayurveda and diet. Americans have embraced eastern medicine, even if not all western doctors have.

I used acupuncture to help me conceive my first child. At the time, I was going to a well known fertility doctor. When I asked him about acupuncture he said, "I've heard it can help people stop smoking, but not get pregnant." Ironically, not all Indian doctors embrace eastern medicine, either. I've met many Indian doctors who also doubt the effectiveness of acupuncture and other non-traditional therapies.

. . .

What should Indian doctors know about practicing medicine in America?

I am told that doctors are gods in India. Their opinions are not questioned. As one doctor described it, "In India, the doctor makes the treatment decisions. In America, the doctor gives the patient options so that the patient can decide."

Respect for doctors in the U.S. has declined. Anyone can access medical information online, so people self diagnose before consulting a doctor. Patients challenge and question their doctor's opinion. In fact, American patients are taught to be their own advocates. The system is complicated and disjointed and a failure to do your own research and ask the right questions can be fatal.

Lawsuits brought against doctors for malpractice and insurance fraud also weaken public trust in the medical profession. In the past, doctors were manipulated by wealthy pharmaceutical companies trying to push new products on patients. The relationship between "drug reps" and doctors is now more closely regulated.

Doctors in America must spend time talking to the family of the patient. They must explain the diagnosis and treatment in non-medical terms. Doctors must also spend time answering questions from the family in a caring and compassionate manner. I am told this is different than in India, where doctors are not expected to explain procedures to a patient's family or answer their questions.

An older doctor, now in his seventies, noted that doctors are treated much more informally in America than in India. While doctors are highly respected in India, in America the patient challenges the doctor and even calls the doctor "doc." Nurses sometimes give orders to doctors. Just like any employee, a doctor has to be careful what he says. Doctors can be terminated for offensive or insensitive language. There are sites online where patients can post negative reviews of doctors. These types of reviews can harm a doctor's reputation.

American doctors must electronically document their patient notes. Many doctors spend hours typing notes into the computer. For older doctors, this is a major burden. Those who cannot type quickly use voice dictation, but it is still time consuming.

One Indian doctor told me that in America, he was recognized and rewarded for his work, but in India he suffered discrimination based on his caste and skin color. This doctor did experience two incidents of prejudice in America, which I share below. In general, however, Indian doctors are regarded as high quality in the U.S.

During his residency, this Indian doctor had a patient ask for a white doctor. The Indian doctor explained that there were no white doctors on duty at that time, which was the truth. The patient realized her only chance at treatment was with the Indian doctor, and let him examine her. This is not common, especially in diverse, urban areas.

The other incident shared by this doctor is more comical than serious. Upon seeing the doctor's brown skin, his patient called the hospital police to report a terrorist was in her room. When the police arrived they all had a good laugh, except for the patient, who they realized was not mentally sound. While these two incidents happened to the same doctor, his other patients have appreciated his care and not shown any signs of prejudice.

One female Indian doctor told me that she is usually mistaken for a nurse, even when she is wearing her white coat and doctor badge.

This same female doctor offered advice for medical residents from outside America. She advised against viewing patients through the eyes of Indian customs. She said to understand your patients you have to understand American behavior and norms. She shared a story about a study partner who had been in America for eight years. They were studying for Part III of the American Medical Licensing Exam, which tests a doctor's interview and diagnosis skills. Her study partner refused to ask the patient if she was sexually active. Since the patient was not married, the student assumed she was not sexually active. The student ignored that in America it is common to have sex without marriage, even when this was explained to him. Not only would this hurt him on the exam, but as a doctor he would not have critical facts for diagnosis. If you are going to practice medicine in a country, you need to understand its people.

. . .

What do doctors need to know about medical billing?

It is no surprise that "medical billing" is a profession in America. Medical offices and hospitals depend on these professionals. The rules and coding categories for insurance reimbursement are so intricate that many doctors do not understand them. Medical billers are often on the phone most of the day, fighting with insurance companies to cover services provided in the office. If you don't work in private practice, you don't have to understand the insurance rules because the hospital handles billing. One doctor admitted to me that her only understanding of insurance is the personal insurance policy she has from her employer (the hospital). When it comes to her patients, she doesn't ask about insurance and doesn't get involved in payment. The good news for private practitioners is you can hire people to handle this onerous task - there are plenty medical billers out there in the workforce!

American doctors are required to keep electronic medical records on patients, which means they can spend hours a week typing up notes about patient visits. Most doctors do this themselves, and often after hours. The staff is too busy with billing and scheduling to assist with these duties, and doctors are the most familiar with the various codes and terms used in the data entry templates.

How are doctors trained in America?

This is a major difference between India and America. In America, students interested in medicine must first complete four years of college, then apply to medical school. Most medical school applicants are rejected; less than 25% are accepted. This is not the case with other graduate schools. For example, a very bad student interested in law will get into a law school somewhere. Also, just because you can afford to pay for medical school does not mean you will get in. You cannot buy your way in. If you are rejected, you have to improve your application and try again.

Medicine as a career has had a hard time competing with the

quicker and easier paths to wealth found on Wall Street and Silicon Valley. Many top students who may have pursued medicine before the rise of hedge funds and tech companies are now lured to these other fields.

9

MONEY & INVESTING

One financially successful Indian immigrant told me the following: in India, people work hard, but in America, people work smart. Indians rely on salary, but Americans make their money work for them through investments and multiple streams of income.

Making money in America is easy and hard at the same time. Easy, because there are so many opportunities to create wealth. Hard, because despite what you may read or hear, there is no simple "get rich quick" formula.

But why does it look like everyone is rich?

It is an illusion. Americans tend to spend more money than they have, and even worse, show it off to others. The phrase "living beyond your means" refers to living a lifestyle you truly can't afford. So don't feel like you are the only one who can't afford what you see others buying. The truth is they probably can't afford it either.

How are Americans paying for all of this?

Americans live on borrowed money known as credit. The money they are spending is not their money. You'll learn quickly that credit is easy to get in America - too easy. You don't even need to show savings to get a credit card. It's easy to get a credit card, but hard to pay off the debt you may build up by using it.

A credit card is not free money. There is a minimum amount due every month, and the credit card company charges interest on the balance. If you stop paying, it will be harder for you to get credit again. Don't fall into the credit card trap. Yes, credit cards are necessary, but use them wisely.

Everything seems so expensive in America. How can I possibly get ahead?

Remember what I said at the start of this chapter - Americans work smart. Time is a limited resource, and there are only so many hours a person can work. Some Americans love to say, "I make money when I'm sleeping." How is this possible? Well, consider this book. It is selling (hopefully!) while I am sleeping or writing my next book. Or consider an investment in a local business - you can be working your regular job while that business is making money for you. The same is true with stocks - they are going up (and down) in value while you are doing other things. This is what Americans mean when they say to make your money work for you. You shouldn't rely on these secondary streams of income for your basic needs, but over time they will help you build wealth beyond what you can earn from your salary alone.

What is a good credit score and how do I get one?

Using credit in a responsible way is important to building wealth. To get a loan you will need to build credit. The easiest way to build good credit is to pay off credit card expenses every month. If you can only afford to pay the minimum, then pay that. The main thing is do not miss a payment. This is true for any expense - school, car loan, rent, cable or electricity. If you miss a payment, your credit score will go down. If you consistently pay on time, your credit score will be strong. There are websites you can use to check your credit score.

How is the U.S. stock market different than the Indian stock market?

The U.S. stock market is one of the most mature and stable markets in the world. It is heavily regulated by the government through the U.S. Security and Exchange Commission. The branch of law governing financial transactions is called "securities law." Beyond government regulation, the U.S. stock market is closely monitored by a financial industry consisting of analysts, lawyers, reporters, bankers and investors. There are scandals and abuses, but it is not nearly as risky as investing in the Indian stock market.

Indian immigrants tell me that the Indian stock market is similar to gambling, and brokers are often corrupt, shady figures. One immigrant called brokers in India "*dalali.*" That is not the case in America, where investing information is readily available and transparent, the government regulates the markets, and people can directly invest without the help of a broker.

Is investing in the stock market just for the rich?

"You have to have money to make money." This is a popular American saying, but isn't as true these days.

In the past, you needed a stock broker to buy stocks. The broker had all the knowledge and was heavily relied on by investors. You had to meet your broker in person, and most were white men. Brokers would only give you their time if you had resources to spend - the more money, the more time. It was much harder for average people to invest in the stock market.

Today, if you have a smart phone you can be your own broker. Investing is now part of popular culture - investing books and television shows are popular with regular folks, and experts like Jim Cramer are household names. The technology boom of the 1990's introduced people to terms like "valuation" and "going public." Hot companies turned young whizzes like Mark Zuckerberg and their stockholders into millionaires, and everyone wanted in on the action. After the boom came the bust, as is the cycle of the market. But the boom created a new class of investor - ordinary people.

What is a hedge fund?

Hedge funds are long-term investments because you lock in a set amount of money, usually hundreds of millions of dollars. You give this money to a hedge fund manager and have to wait a few years for the return. The broker might make short-term moves with the money in search of the highest gain, but you do not control the money.

The reason these are called "hedge" funds is because a "hedge" investment is a bet against the market, so the rewards can be extremely profitable.

What is insider trading?

Insider trading is illegal in the U.S. It is the use of "insider" information to buy or sell a stock. "Insider" information is information not known to the public, so using it to invest is an unfair abuse of the market. Martha Stewart, creator of a cooking and lifestyle empire, was convicted of insider trading and spent time in prison. It is a serious offense.

But everyone is looking for a stock tip, right? Isn't the financial industry based on who has the best information about stocks? Yes - but these are not insiders. Basically, everyone is guessing and only the insiders (executives, board members, lawyers and other people closely involved with a company) know the real story. Investing in the stock market is not an exact science. Companies and brokers may try to sell you on the strength of their information and analysis, but nobody has a foolproof way to beat the market. If they say they do, chances are they are insiders and you could go to jail if you act on their advice.

. . .

Is there a real Wall Street?

Yes. Wall Street is located in downtown New York City, but the term refers to the entire U.S. investment industry.

Home ownership seems to be a very important goal for Americans.

In the U.S., home ownership is one of the best ways to build personal wealth. You may not think you can afford to purchase a home until later in your career. Very few Americans buy a home without a mortgage (bank loan). The bank reviews your financials (salary, credit score, savings, other debt) and determine how much to lend you (mortgage). If you do not pay the monthly mortgage bill, the bank can foreclose on the loan and take back the property (collateral).

According to a 2017 study by the Pew Research Center, Asian-Americans are below the national average in home ownership. The study found that 63% of Americans own homes, compared to 57% of Asian-Americans.[1]

I don't want to be in debt, so why would I take a bank loan to buy a house?

This thinking could be one of the explanations for the Pew Research finding that Asian-Americans trail the American average in home ownership. It is hard for some Indian immigrants to be comfortable with being in debt to the bank.

One Indian immigrant explained to me that having a mortgage makes her husband very nervous. Whenever she brings up a new expense, he replies, "But we owe money to the bank!" She will tell him they have a low interest rate on the mortgage, and would be penalized if they paid it off early. She explained to me that saving is more important in India than in America. Back in India, her grandfather used to tell her, "Whether you have two rupees or two million rupees, what matters is how much you save."

Debt should not be feared as long as you can "afford" the debt. There is a responsible way to take on debt, and sometimes it is the right financial choice. For example, even if you have the money to pay for a house in full, you may want to use this money for other investments or expenses. "Carrying" a mortgage also shows future lenders that you can handle credit, which is important.

Is investing in real estate a smart investment?

Over time property values usually go up, but the question is how long you are willing to wait. You may hear talk about "flipping" homes - this means buying a property with the goal of selling it for more than the purchase price. This only works when prices are rising. Most investors "buy and hold" property for the long term. If the rental income pays the mortgage and expenses, the owner can hold the property until the price is right to sell.

You can become wealthy from real estate investments, but like any investment, there is risk. Leading up to the 2008 financial crisis, banks gave mortgages too easily. Some of these mortgages were "no money down" deals, so borrowers could purchase homes beyond their means and delay payments. When the mortgages came due, the system collapsed and home values are only now starting to regain the value they had before 2008.

What should I know about being a landlord?

It is hard work, inconvenient and expensive. Many Americans don't want to get their "hands dirty" with real estate investing for this reason. One investor told me he prefers stocks to real estate because a stock isn't going to call him in the middle of the night with a broken toilet. Those who decide to be landlords may use a real estate management company to handle repairs and rent collection, even though it means giving up a percentage of the profit.

Tenants have rights in America. There are "legal aid" lawyers who represent low income tenants for free. Even a tenant who has not paid rent may have defenses excusing nonpayment. You should be familiar with landlord/tenant law if you are going to be a landlord. You will also need to know about the various government agencies that regulate and subsidize rental housing in America. Especially in cities, housing is heavily regulated and violators are fined.

How is running a business different in the U.S. than India?

Indian business owners I spoke with feel that running a business in America is much easier than in India. In their home country, these Indians say that business is about who you know, not the quality of the service or product you are selling. In America, businesses are regulated by state and local laws, so everyone is following the same rules.

It is common practice to form a corporation in America, no matter how small the company may be. This does not mean you are running a multinational corporation, or intend to build one. Incorporation is about asset protection. If the business is sued, the only asset at risk are the assets held by the corporation. Your home and any personal savings are safe. America is a very litigious society, meaning people are quick to file lawsuits.

What do I need to know about running my own business?

It's not possible to just set up shop and open your business without first taking steps required for all businesses by your state and local government. You can find these requirements on your state website. Keep in mind that you will probably need a license to do what you are planning to do. Some licenses are easier to get than others. Some just require paperwork, others, like the license to practice law, require specialized training and a certification exam.

Once you incorporate, your company will be a separate entity under the law. You will have to keep the records for this company separate from your personal records, and file taxes for this entity each year. A good accountant should be able to help you with book-keeping and tax planning.

If you are hiring employees, be careful. As we discussed in earlier chapters, it is very easy for employees to file discrimination claims, so watch what you say. Also, if you are building a legitimate business, don't hire workers "off the books." America doesn't have the supply of cheap labor found in India, and it is illegal to hire children. Those willing to work for less may not be here legally. As an employer, you have to ask for proof of status, but do not have to verify it (at least in New York - this is state specific). Still, if you want to be taken seriously by banks and customers and don't want to risk fines, be careful who you hire.

What should I know about running a cash business?

Some think that running a cash business gives them freedom from state regulations and taxes. If it isn't on paper, they think, how would the government find out about it?

The I.R.S. can audit your business at any time. If it finds that you are underreporting your income, it will not only impose taxes on the underreported amount, but could also hit you with a fine.

Like any other business, a cash business can't overlook sales tax. Make sure you charge sales tax on every sale, and set that money aside to pay to the state when taxes are due.

What is a franchise?

Indians are often associated with franchise businesses such as Dunkin' Donuts, 7-11 and Subway. Buying a franchise does not make you the owner of the business. You are the franchisee, and the owner is the franchisor. As the franchisee, you have very little freedom to run the business as you wish. You can't even set the prices. One Indian franchisee told me the franchisor spies on the stores to make sure they are following the franchisor's rules on customer service, product display and countless other details. Also keep in mind that the franchisor will not buy the business back from you. So you could be stuck running a failing business until you can find a buyer.

You may find banking much easier in the U.S. than in India.

It may seem like every street corner in America has a bank, right next to a pizza place and nail salon. It's probably one of the first things you'll notice about banking here. These banks compete for customers, which means better customer service and deals for you. Banking is also regulated by the government, bringing a level of standardization across different banks.

Some Indian immigrants shared with me confusion about the changes in bank names. There is no major bank in America, like the State Bank of India. Banks in America are bought and sold frequently and change names and logos when they do. This can be unsettling to an Indian immigrant used to the stability of the State Bank of India.

What is social security?

This federal program takes a percentage from your paycheck and returns it to you later in life. Currently, the earliest age you can collect Social Security is 62.

Every election year candidates warn that the Social Security fund is heading for bankruptcy. This is because politicians have used the Social Security fund for other purposes.

So why do I need to save for retirement if I pay for Social Security?

Social security is not enough for most people to live on.

What is life insurance?

Life insurance is insurance on your life - meaning that if you die, the insurance company pays money to your survivors (beneficiaries). Of course, you have to pay monthly premiums to get this benefit.

Why would someone do this? It isn't just to plan for the unexpected and take care of your loved ones after you are gone - the truth is it's expensive to die in America. Death brings funeral expenses, unpaid debts and taxes. Even with this reality, life insurance can still be a hard sell in America. Many people would rather have the money now than plan for the future.

Do I need a will?

Yes. Yes. Yes. If you die without a will in the U.S., the state government will decide how to divide your assets based on the laws of your state.

What is estate planning?

You may hear the term "estate planning." This is not for people with estates - it refers to planning for your assets (estate) after you die. Creating a will is part of this, as is life insurance and other forms of planning to minimize the estate tax (also known as the death tax).

What is a "non-profit" or 501(c)(3) organization?

"Non-profit" doesn't mean the organization makes no profit. These types of organizations can make a profit, but the money must be used for one of the specific purposes designated in Section 501(c)(3) of the U.S. Tax Code. Some examples are churches, schools and charities. The I.R.S. determines which organizations meet the requirements for "non-profit" status.

10

TAXES

A popular saying in America is, "The only thing certain in life is death and taxes." Americans avoid talking about death, but not taxes. Taxes are always a big topic in political elections, and the subject of endless books, courses, articles and debates. There's even a "tax season" just like any sport season. Much of American life revolves around taxes.

What are the arguments for and against raising taxes?

Here are some common points of difference in the tax debate:

- Taxes are too high and money should remain with the people. Others argue that in order for the government to provide services (and expand these services) the government needs more money.
- Government waste and inefficiency is a reason not to raise taxes. People are better judges of how to spend their own money than the government.
- The rich do not pay their fair share of taxes. Others

point out that the poor pay no taxes at all and most taxes are collected from the rich.

- Reducing corporate taxes helps the economy because corporations will use the savings for investment and expansion. Others argue that reducing corporate taxes only causes corporations to keep more profits.

So what is the secret to paying low taxes in America?

Every American taxpayer suspects everyone else is paying lower taxes, or has the secret to minimize taxes. The secret is that there is no secret.

Tax planning and strategies exist, but there is no secret to beat the tax collector. Some types of income are taxed lower than others, and the government gives tax benefits to activities it wants to encourage, like home ownership.

When is the "tax season?"

For federal and state income tax, the "tax season" begins when employers send out W-2 statements and ends at midnight on April 15, when taxes are due. Property taxes are collected by local governments, usually twice a year.

Is this the only time of year I can pay my taxes?

Extensions are possible, but you have to pay an estimate of what you think you owe by the April 15 deadline.

What is taxable income?

The most common income includes salary, investment income, rental income and interest from a bank account. Even children can have tax liability for investments made in their name.

. . .

How are taxes calculated?

For income taxes, federal and state governments use a graduated tax system, which means that increasing levels of income are taxed at higher rates. These levels are called "tax brackets" and there are seven brackets in the federal income tax system. The rate is only applied to the amount of income in the bracket. In 2018, the lowest tax bracket was 10% for income up to $9,525 and the highest bracket was 37% for income over $500,000.

Property taxes are a set percentage applied to the value of your home. Home values are assessed periodically, and you can challenge the value assigned to your home by filing a "grievance" with your local tax authority.

Sales or excise taxes are a set percentage charged when you pay for an item. It is up to the vendor to collect this tax.

Why do I hear people say the rich don't pay their fair share of taxes?

If you make a lot of income, you have to pay taxes based on your bracket. The way the rich pay low taxes is because they make money in ways other than income. For example, money from real estate and certain types of investments are taxed at a lower rate. Some people say the people who pay the least tax are those who have the money to pay accountants and lawyers to read and understand the tax code (over 1,000 pages long) and find the legal "loop holes."

What taxes do I have to pay?

Federal Income Tax

Due April 15th, graduated tax based on income, separated into seven tax brackets.

State Income Tax

In 2018, the state with the highest income tax was California (13.3%), and seven states have no state income tax (Florida is one of them). Amounts paid in state income tax can be used as a deduction against your federal taxable income.

Federal and State Excise Taxes

Taxes on specific items paid at time of consumption. One example is tobacco (cigarettes). There is a federal and state excise tax on each pack of cigarettes sold.

Local Property Tax

Property tax is a percentage of the assessed value of your property. You can file a grievance with your town to challenge this assessed value. In 2018, the state with the highest property tax was New Jersey (1.89%) and the lowest was Louisiana (.18%). These rates are averages of the tax rates in the towns, since property tax is a local and not state tax.

Local/City Tax

Some local governments and cities also collect income taxes, but not all.

Sales/Consumption Tax

Taxes collected when a sale is made. Five states have no sales tax. Some states offer "tax holidays" - days when no sales tax is charged throughout the state.

Estate "Death" Tax

Tax on assets left behind when you die.

If I am working for an Indian company while I am in America, do I pay taxes to the U.S. government on that income?

This depends on the type of visa you hold. Green card holders must pay U.S. taxes. If you hold a non-immigrant visa and remain in the U.S. for at least 31 days in the current tax year or 183 days total in the past three years, you will most likely have to pay taxes in the U.S.

If I am making money in India while I am in America, do I pay taxes to the U.S. government on that income?

If you are a green card holder or otherwise required to pay taxes in the U.S., you must report all worldwide income for the year, not just income earned in the U.S.

What happens if I don't pay taxes?

The U.S. government is serious about collecting taxes. Not paying taxes or lying on your taxes is the federal crime of "tax evasion." Famous Americans have gone to prison for this crime. The main way the I.R.S. discovers tax evasion is through an audit, but people can also report evasion to the I.R.S. So pay your taxes and keep records to document your tax statement in case you are ever audited.

Can I prepare my taxes myself or do I need an accountant?

People with simple finances can probably file their own taxes. By "simple" I mean you are a W-2 employee (you are not self-employed) and do not have investments. Every tax season you will see new tax programs for sale that calculate your taxes and even submit them to the I.R.S. with a few clicks. Once you start investing and building your own business, taxes can get complicated. Not all money is treated equally by the tax code, and a trained accountant will know the smartest strategies for minimizing your tax liability.

But I heard that some people pay no taxes?

People below a certain income level do not pay income tax, but they still pay sales tax and property tax could be included in their rent.

Should taxes be taken out of my paycheck if I am not a citizen?

If you are in the U.S. on an A, D, F, J, M, Q, or G visa, you are exempt from F.I.C.A. tax (Social Security and Medicare) and this tax should not be deducted from your paycheck. Years ago, my mother-in-law pointed this out to her employer, a major American credit card company, and the human resources department had no idea what she was talking about. I'm confident companies are now aware of this exemption. If not, do not be afraid to tell them - the I.R.S. website has a clear explanation you can refer them to.

If money is deducted from my paycheck all year for taxes, why do I have to pay again in April?

For most workers, the amount deducted is less than what you owe. However, if you deducted more than you owe in taxes, you will actually receive money back from the government.

What does the government do with tax money?

There is a joke that the federal government is basically an army and an insurance company. This is because most of the federal budget is spent on military and health insurance programs (Medicare, Medicaid and health insurance subsidies under the Affordable Care Act). On the state level, tax money is mostly used for schools and the police.

11

GOVERNMENT & LAWS

You are coming to America at a highly political time. Everything is politicized - even your very presence here is political. Many of us try to avoid political talk, but it's not easy. The 24 hours news cycle is relentless, and politics has now crept into the worlds of sports, business and entertainment.

Putting politics aside, Americans have a love/hate relationship with government. They know they need it, but they don't want too much of it. The American "Founding Fathers" revolted against an overbearing monarchy. The Constitution is based on the belief that a government left unchecked would oppress its citizens. That is why we have checks and balances and the bill of rights, as well as other clauses in the Constitution that protect citizens from their own government.

***People say America is a nation of laws. Isn't every nation?
How is American law different?***

Respect for the rule of law is ultimately why our system works. Americans are equal before the law. Sure, the wealthy have greater access to lawmakers and legal representation, and we could do a better job enforcing the law equally. But overall, people have confidence in the law. It's why there are so many lawsuits in our country. If there was no faith in the courts, people would not use them. It's also why contracts are obeyed, workers show up to work and people in general follow through on their obligations.

How does voter participation in the U.S. compare to India?

With all the political talk, it's surprising more Americans don't vote. The percentage of Indians voting in the 2014 Indian general election was higher than the percentage of Americans voting in the 2016 presidential election. By most measures, 58% of Americans voted in the 2016 election. Indian percentages are ranked by state - the lowest turnout in the 2014 general election was 49.5% (Jammu and Kashmir) and the highest was 86.61% (Lakshadweep).

Who can vote in America?

The founding fathers wrote that "all men are created equal," but many citizens did not have the right to vote until the 20th century. The 19th amendment granted women the right to vote in 1920. The 15th amendment gave freed male slaves the right to vote in 1870, but in reality blacks in the South were blocked from voting until the Voting Rights Act of 1965. Native Americans could not legally vote until 1924. Chinese immigrants were given the right to vote in 1943.

Only citizens eighteen and older can vote. A green card holder cannot vote. Once you are a citizen, you must register to vote in the state where you reside. You cannot show up to vote without registering in advance. In many states, you can register to vote online. Convicted criminals are prohibited from voting when they are in jail and after they are released.

Is this really how Americans vote?

I bet you will be shocked to see how Americans elect our president. Long lines are common, the election monitors are usually elderly volunteers, and the actual voting machines are outdated. It is unbelievable for such a wealthy and technologically advanced country to elect its leaders in this way. Some states ask voters to poke holes in cardboard cards, or fill in circles with a black marker and run it through a scanning machine (this was how I voted in 2016).

Sadly, there is a history in America of making it harder for groups to vote, instead of enabling greater voter participation. Literacy tests, taxes, grandfather clauses, intimidation and property ownership requirements kept blacks from voting after the Civil War.

For this reason, restrictions on voting are viewed with skepticism. Some recent restrictions have taken the form of requiring voter identification cards and limited voting hours. As a busy working mom and concerned citizen, I want voting to be as easy and accessible as possible. Some states allow early voting for up to two weeks before Election Day. This makes sense to me.

When is Election Day and what is on the ballot?

Legalization of marijuana, gay marriage, affirmative action at public universities and even whether to split California into three states are some issue that citizens vote on. These are called "referendums" and are popular in some states (California, especially) as a way for people to rule directly on an issue.

Election Day is always the first Tuesday in November. The president is elected every four years, senators every six years and representatives every two. State and local officials are also elected on Election Day, as are some judges. If you will not be in your local district on Election Day, you can mail in a paper absentee ballot.

What is gerrymandering?

This is the practice of drawing the map for a Congressional district to favor one party. If a Congressional district is 75% Democrat, what incentive does the representative have to ever work with Republicans in Congress, or listen to Republicans in the district?

Some blame this manipulation of the district maps for the extreme views of politicians because if they represent a mix of views they will be more likely to compromise.

What is the Electoral College?

This is not a university for politicians, although many of them would benefit from more time in school.

In order to win the presidential election, a candidate must win more than 270 of the 538 electors. When a candidate wins the popular vote in a state, it wins either all or a share of the electors from that state. The number of electors granted to each state is the sum of the state's senators and Congressional representatives. In recent history, both Hillary Clinton and Al Gore won the popular vote, but not a majority of the electors.

The electoral college ensures that our president is not selected on popular vote alone. The founding fathers sought to protect the voice of smaller states in the process. Otherwise, the president could just win with the votes of major cities, and the rest of the country would not have a say in the process or, more importantly, the ear of the president.

What are the primaries?

Living in America can feel like a never ending presidential election. This is partly because of the primary process. All possible candidates run in primary elections in every state of the country. It begins a year before Election Day, but candidates must campaign (and raise funds) in all fifty states for months leading up to the primary elections.

Just like with the electoral college, the primary process is another protection for the influence of smaller states. The first two primary states are Iowa and New Hampshire. As a result, candidates spend time, effort and resources to win in these primaries. Without their status as first in the country primaries, it is doubtful many presidential candidates would campaign heavily in Iowa or New Hampshire.

. . .

What is the role of the U.S. Supreme Court?

The Supreme Court is the final say on any Constitutional dispute. Cases unrelated to the Constitution are heard in lower federal or state courts. Supreme Court justices are appointed by the president for life, but must be confirmed by Congress. There are only nine, so each appointment is important to the balance of views on the Court and the president's legacy. Landmark Supreme Court cases such as *Brown vs. Board of Education* (school desegregation), *Loving vs. Virginia* (interracial marriage) and *Bush v. Gore* (deciding the 2000 election) have transformed our society.

What is original intent?

Since the Indian Constitution was written in 1950, it may seem odd that anyone would try to view the words of our governing document through the eyes of men who lived over two hundred years ago. This is the meaning of "original intent" - a manner of interpreting the Constitution through the meaning intended by those who wrote it in 1787. It is a conservative view.

Others view the Constitution as a living document that should grow and be interpreted by the society we are living in, not the past. The liberal justices on the Supreme Court follow this interpretation.

What is jury duty?

One Indian doctor immigrant admitted he did not register to vote because he did not want to be called for jury duty. When he complains about politics we tell him, "If you didn't vote you can't complain!"

When you hear that a case was decided by "a jury of one's peers," where do you think those peers come from? They are you and me (if you are a citizen). India abolished the jury system, but jury trials are common in America.

It begins when you receive a letter requiring you to appear at the court house for jury duty. Just because you show up doesn't mean you will be selected by the lawyers to serve on the jury. In fact, chances are low that you will be picked. If you are selected, you will be paid a small amount and can't talk to anyone about the case until it is over. Employers understand jury duty is a legal obligation and do not penalize workers for missed days. You can postpone jury duty for certain reasons.

There are tricks to not being picked, based on the type of case before the court. For example, a lawyer suing a doctor may not want a doctor on the jury.

How do the wars in Iraq and Afghanistan affect life in America?

America has been at war in Afghanistan since 2001 and Iraq since 2003. The costs of these wars are now in the trillions, when the interest on borrowed money is factored in. To the average American, these wars are strangely accepted as a fact of life. The money spent isn't questioned, and Americans are not demanding the wars be justified or ended. They just go on...

Less than half a percent of the American population is active duty military (in 2017, 2% of the U.S. military was Asian). Military service is voluntary. America has not had a military draft since 1973. Unless you live near a military base, you may not meet military families in your daily life. Still, they exist. Multiple deployments to Iraq and Afghanistan have resulted in greater burdens on these families. Returning veterans suffer from depression, brain injury and post traumatic stress disorder (PTSD). These are often silent sufferers; the wars linger on as most Americans live their lives largely unaffected.

Are Indian-Americans Democrats or Republicans?

Indian-Americans voted overwhelming for Hillary Clinton in the 2016 election - over 70% voted for Clinton and less than 20% voted for Trump.

. . .

Who are some notable Indian-Americans in American politics?

Several Indian-Americans are serving high-level posts in the Trump administration, and there are currently five Indian-Americans serving in Congress (one senator, four representatives, all Democrats).

Nikki Haley is the first Indian-American female appointed to a presidential cabinet position. She served as U.S. Ambassador to the United Nations from 2016 until 2018. In 2011, she became the second Indian-American governor of a U.S. state (South Carolina). Haley was raised Sikh and is now a Christian. Her family is from Amristar, India.

Kamala Harris was elected the first female and first Asian-American Attorney General of California. She is now a senator from California, the state's first senator of Indian-American descent. She is of Tamil and Jamaican ancestry. She has announced that she is running for president in 2020.

In 2007, Bobby Jindal became the first Indian-American governor of a U.S. state (Louisiana). Jindal's ancestry is Punjabi. He was raised Hindu, but converted to Christianity.

Who were the "founding fathers"?

We've talked about their work throughout this chapter, but who were they?

First is George Washington, not just because he was the first president, but because he didn't let himself become a king. He only served two terms, even though there was no term limit in the Constitution. Every other president after him followed this unwritten rule, except for Franklin D. Roosevelt. Washington was also a general in the Revolutionary War. Thomas Jefferson is probably the second most famous founding father. Jefferson drafted the Declaration of Independence, was a notable inventor, served as the third president and founded the University of Virginia. James

Madison was the fourth president and one of the three authors of The Federalist Papers, which explained the Constitution to the country. Alexander Hamilton was an author of The Federalist Papers and founder of the National Bank. He has risen in popularity because of the Broadway musical named after him. The elder statesman of the group is Benjamin Franklin. We may not have won the Revolutionary War if Franklin didn't win French support. He was an inventor, writer, founder of the public library system, the post office and the University of Pennsylvania.

Washington, Jefferson and Madison were slave owners. The history of slavery in America is a gruesome, unjust and sad story. No one was untouched by it, even our esteemed leaders who wrote so eloquently about freedom and equality of all men.

How is President Trump different than other American presidents?

Trump is the first president to have no political or military experience. A doctor tenant in a building owned by Trump's father diagnosed Trump with a bone spur so he could be excused from serving in the Vietnam War.

The only other president who did not hold political office or serve in the military was Herbert Hoover - but Hoover did have government experience. Hoover was the U.S. Secretary of Commerce and led the U.S. Food Administration prior to running for president. The stock market crashed after Hoover became president in 1929. The nation suffered under the Great Depression, and Hoover was a one term president. Americans should have learned that experience matters for one of the most important jobs in the world. None of us would be hired without experience - shouldn't we expect the same for our leader?

Trump is not the first Hollywood character to be elected president. Ronald Reagan was an actor, but he was the governor of California before running for president.

During the 2016 presidential campaign, Trump was disrespectful to his fellow Republican nominees. He was childish and unprepared in debates. His crude, boastful and uninformed statements are below the standard set by American presidents. No other candidate would have survived after mocking a disabled reporter, criticizing a female candidate's looks, or after the release of a tape in which Trump bragged about grabbing women's private parts. Few Republicans abandoned him, perhaps because they need him to implement their economic and social policies.

Trump's "America first" world view is a departure from past American presidents. His characterization of the press as an "enemy" undermines what our founding fathers declared necessary for a vital democracy. His loyalty to North Korea and Russia is unprecedented, and contradicts advice from his own government. Misleading, demeaning "tweets" were not sent by past presidents. As a lawyer, I can say he does not understand the Constitution or respect the rule of law in America. As part of an immigrant family, I can say he does not understand the immigration process. As a white woman, I can say he does not know the racial history of this country, or value women for their full abilities.

I think you get the picture. He is not like past presidents. I am hopeful, though. Americans will not abandon their standards forever.

Why is the slogan "Make America Great Again" controversial?

Every country wants to be great. It's the "again" part that scares people. It is scary because there are ugly and painful chapters in American history. In these chapters, Americans denied political, economic and social power to blacks, immigrants and other minorities. The white majority profited from an unfair system. Some fear this is what Trump supporters are referring to as "great" and what they want to restore.

12

WHERE TO LIVE

I recently read in a local newspaper that between 1980 and 2010, the Asian population on Long Island increased by 518%. According to the article, this explosion of Asian immigrants on Long Island was very positive because they brought money, new businesses and good students to the island. Just drive through the town of Hicksville and you'll see the proof. When I was growing up, Hicksville was a white, forgotten town. Now, it is lined with Indian, Chinese and Korean grocery stores, restaurants, dress shops and tutoring centers.

How do I know if a place is friendly to Indian immigrants?

The easy answer is to say that most immigrant friendly areas are found in cities or towns surrounding cities (suburbs). These areas are ethnically diverse, which forces groups to co-exist. Some signs that an area is friendly to Indian immigrants are:

- Indian owned businesses

- Celebration of Indian festivals (Diwali is the most known in the U.S.) sponsored by the town and local groups, and the events are well attended

- Local Indian community groups - look for websites and social media pages to see how active they are

- Indian students in the schools. In some districts, parents have petitioned for schools to be closed on Diwali, and won. Schools that are closed for Diwali would have a high number of Indian students.

- Indian leadership in government. You can find names of town officials on the town's website. Some towns even have a diversity officer.

- How are stories about immigrants discussed in the newspaper or online? For example, discussions of Indians in Hicksville are overwhelmingly positive.

- Have there been any hate crimes towards Indians, or immigrants? You can get this information from the police office.

What are other signs of a good neighborhood?

Many Indians want to live near educated and professional people. Check out the local library - is it crowded on the weekends? Does it have programs for children? Living near a university brings a diverse group of educated people, as well as educational and cultural programs for families. What are the main industries in the town and closest city? See if there is a good mix of family activities in the town, not just sports.

. . .

Where do most Indians live in the U.S.?

Some Indian immigrant communities are legendary - Jackson Heights in Queens, Edison in New Jersey, Devon Street in Chicago. According to the 2010 census, the states with the highest population of Indians are: California, New York, New Jersey and Texas.

The largest percentage of Asian-Americans live on the West coast, with one third in California. Only 12% of Asian-Americans live in the Midwest, 23% live in the South (including New Jersey), and 20% live in the Northeast.

Do I want to live in a predominantly Indian area?

Immigrants I spoke with said living in a majority Indian area makes it harder to learn American customs and integrate into American society.

What are the positives and negatives of living in a strong school district?

Most will say there are no negatives, because the children will receive a great education. Even with this great education, it could be more difficult for your child to get into a top college because these colleges do not accept more than one or two students from each school. So the schools (and parents!) are highly competitive in these districts. This could affect the quality of life for you and your kid.

That said, it is still better to live in a strong school district. As more people are learning, going to a "top" college is not where students will necessarily get the best education, and there are many strong schools that are not ranked in the top ten. Getting into a top ten college has in many ways become a game of chance and is not based on merit - sports, wealth, connections and race play a big role. If you and your child can tune out the misguided competition from other families, you will be fine in a strong school district.

One more consideration is that you want your kid to be in an environment where academic excellence is encouraged, and even "cool." There are many distractions in high school, and some schools emphasize sports and social life over academics. You don't want your kid to have to choose between being smart and fitting in.

Why is living with parents uncommon in America?

For many Americans, living with parents or grandparents is a sign that something didn't go as planned. The common belief is that adult children should be living on their own. When you see this arrangement, it is usually because the adult children are out of work or can't afford to buy a home. They are not living with their parents by choice.

This is not true for Indian immigrants. Living with family makes the transition to America easier. Most immigrants tell me they prefer to live with family when they arrive. The family provides food and shelter, companionship and guidance.

What is all this I hear about blue and red states?

"There is no red America. There is no blue America. There is one America."

This is one of Barrack Obama's most famous quotes. It is from his keynote speech at the 2004 Democratic Convention. This speech made him a celebrity overnight. The colors mean that a state voted Democratic (blue) or Republican (red). Unfortunately, we still talk about red and blue states, but now there is also talk of purple states - those where it is hard to predict which way a state will vote.

Is there a North/South divide?

Imagine India and Pakistan trying to exist as one country after the brutality of the Partition. That is what happened in the U.S. after the Civil War between the North and South.

It is estimated that 620,000 Americans died in the Civil War, compared to 644,000 Americans that died in all other wars combined. It was a horrific loss of life, and the end of slavery destroyed the Southern economy. The Southern states are the poorest states in the country. Southerners are mocked as uneducated "red necks." Some Southerners call the Civil War the "War of Northern Aggression" and proudly wave the Confederate flag.

Where are the Hindu temples in America?

Yes, there are grand, beautiful temples built in areas with open land, and simpler temples in cities. The big temples are often in places Indians visit, and the smaller, simpler temples are in urban centers where Indians live their daily lives. The mandirs in populated areas are on busy streets and from the outside you can't tell that it is a temple.

Are there places for my children to learn about Indian culture?

If you live near other Indians, you may find weekly culture, language and dance classes for children. Temples also organize programs for children to meet each other and learn about Hinduism.

Those who do not live around other Indians use books and the Internet for cultural education and language learning.

Is it smart to live in a place with low property taxes?

If you pick a location based on low property taxes you must understand that the resources and services will likely be of a lower quality than in a higher taxed town. The local tax base directly influences the quality of the public schools, library, parks, roads, police and other services.

Even on Long Island, which has strong public schools in general, the schools in districts with high property taxes simply have more money to spend on teachers, enrichment programs, special education, extra-curricular programs, technology and libraries.

. . .

What is housing discrimination?

Housing discrimination is prohibited under federal law. The Fair Housing Act of 1968 outlaws unequal treatment of people seeking housing based on a person's race, national origin (ethnicity), religion, age, disability, gender or family status (type of family - for example, a pregnant single woman or unmarried couple).

What does this mean? The categories listed above can't be the reason a landlord, realtor, bank or home seller denies housing, sets different standards or requirements to buy or rent housing, terminates a tenant, limits the availability of housing or falsely states that housing is unavailable.

Similar to an E.E.O.C. complaint for employment discrimination, a complaint for discriminatory housing can be filed quite easily and without a lawyer. Complaints are filed with the Housing and Urban Development administration.

Why are neighborhoods segregated?

Housing discrimination against black Americans throughout history is one of the reasons neighborhoods are still segregated today. Discrimination was written into home deeds and leases. Houses were sold on the condition that they would not be resold to blacks. After World War II, government loans were given to developers to build planned communities on the condition that the houses were only sold to whites. These discriminatory policies of banks and realtors are known as "redlining."

Levittown was one of these planned communities, and has been celebrated as an ideal, iconic post-war community. I learned about Levittown growing up, like all Long Island kids do. We never learned that it excluded blacks.

How can you say neighborhoods are segregated when there are so many Asians moving into white neighborhoods?

You hear this a lot. "There's no segregation because our town is 50% Asian!"

The major rise of Asian immigration happened after the Fair Housing Act, so the country knew it was a problem and set up a means to address it before most Asian immigrants arrived.

Housing discrimination may not be happening as much to Asians, but it still happens to blacks. Civil rights groups send potential buyers from different races to houses for sale to catch discriminatory practices. Recent lawsuits prove that housing discrimination still exists, even for blacks with good jobs and good credit.

Yes, things are better today. But it's a mistake to look at certain neighborhoods and blame segregation on the people who live there. Don't make the mistake of thinking everything is equal, because for a long time it wasn't and we still see the effects of that today.

13

SOCIAL STATUS IN AMERICA

"All men are created equal." These are perhaps the most famous lines from the Declaration of Independence. Unlike in India, social status is not predetermined in America - it must be earned. Consider our history - we broke from a country where social status was based on birth. The last thing Americans want is a social system that reflects the strict class structures of England.

Of course, there are Americans born into privilege and Americans born into poverty, but the "rags to riches" millionaire is more beloved by Americans than any person born with wealth.

Who are the upper class in America?

In today's America, social status is largely determined by wealth. The rich are the upper class - it does not matter where they come from, who their parents are or how they made their money. Race and ethnicity do not keep people out of the upper class - money matters, period.

The opposite is also true. Anyone can fall into the lower class, even the rich, famous and well connected. In fact, the higher the fall, the more fascinating it is to the American media and public.

Is social status less rigid in America than India?

There are no *brahmins* in America. People from all classes mix together, both socially and at work. Job status does not stop people from talking, eating lunch together or becoming friends. If you don't mix with all types you may be called a "snob" - a negative term for people who act better than others.

One Indian immigrant told me she was surprised to see neighbors form friendships across professional lines - garbage collectors, lawyers, doctors, teachers and policemen treat each other as equals. An Indian doctor who arrived in the 1970s was shocked when the doctors at his lunch table invited a porter to sit with them.

What is FOBI?

Indian immigrants use the term "FOBI" (fresh off the boat) to describe Indians who are new to America and not yet familiar with its customs. Other Asian immigrant groups use the term as well. There is even an American television show about a Chinese family called "Fresh Off the Boat."

What is "class warfare"?

From listening to the news and political candidates you would think Americans blame the "top 1%" wealthiest Americans for their country's problems. Democrats argue that taxes should be raised on the highest earners. You will hear calls for these wealthy Americans to "pay their fair share."

The numbers tell a different story. For the 2017 tax year, the top 1% paid a greater share of federal taxes collected than the bottom 90% of income earners combined. The top 50% of all taxpayers paid 97% of taxes collected. About half of low income earners don't pay any taxes at all. The wealthy often ask why they are under attack when they are funding the country.

Where do you see class division in America?

Class division happens in housing and education. In America, property taxes fund local education. This is not the case in most countries. As a result, wealthy neighborhoods have better financed schools. Access to expensive private universities is often limited to wealthy students. The practice of favoring applicants from "legacy" families only widens the class division at these colleges. Legacies are discussed later in this book.

Does family history matter in America?

It's common to hear Indians talk about a person's family. A potential marriage partner must come from a "good" family. Americans don't really talk that way. Individuals are not judged based on their family. To most Americans, good people can come from bad families and bad people can come from good families.

If you do come from a respected family, I wouldn't share this with others. Nobody wants to hear that your parents are doctors, engineers or bankers. This will only turn people against you. They may even think you do not have any accomplishments of your own to speak of. You are expected to make your own way in America.

Think of the American billionaires Jeff Bezos, Bill Gates, Mark Zuckerberg, Warren Buffet and Sam Walton (Walmart) - they were raised in upper middle class or middle class families, not elite, famous known families. Three of those billionaires have pledged to donate their wealth to charity and not leave it to their descendants, claiming that inheriting wealth can hurt more than help future generations.

Are Indians in America still affected by the caste system?

According to Indians I have interviewed, the Indian caste system does still show up among Indian immigrants. Other Indians might ask where you are from and different regional groups might not mix as much of those from the same place. My husband's family is from Bihar, and some cousins have told me that Indians from New Delhi, Mumbai and wealthier parts of India treat them differently because of this.

14

RACE IN AMERICA

The other chapters in this book will hopefully be helpful for you, but this one is more than that. Understanding America's racial history will help America.

I hear many successful immigrants deny that there is inequality of opportunity in America. They say, "I made it here, so anyone can" or "America is a place where you can succeed if you just work hard." To an Indian immigrant, this is probably true. Inequality in India is much more rigid and deeply entrenched than any inequality in America. Caste, poverty and gender limit opportunities for Indians to a greater degree than race does for Americans.

But America is not India, and just because opportunity is more available in America does not mean it is available to all.

What you see in front of you - crime on the news, bad neighborhoods, broad income and education gaps - it's easy to blame this on the people and say they just haven't worked as hard as you. In this chapter, I'm asking you to consider that what you see in front of you is not the whole story. We only learn half of history, and it is the history written by the dominant group. The other half of history plays a role in what you see today.

America is starting to recognize this. It's important to continue this important conversation and move it forward. Saying you just have to work hard to make it in America shuts it down.

Slavery wasn't just in the South.

This is a popular misconception in America. I never learned in school that slavery existed outside of the South. I grew up on Long Island and never knew the history of slavery on Long Island. While the North did not have the plantations of the South, slaves helped with fishing, households and farming. In 1776, the year the Revolutionary War began, New York had about 20,000 slaves. Slave auctions were common on Wall Street in New York City. Slavery was abolished in New York in 1827, thirty-four years before the Civil War began.

What happened to black Americans after the Civil War?

When the Civil War ended, there were about four million freed slaves in the South. In some states, such as South Carolina, the freed slave population outnumbered whites. President Lincoln was assassinated in April 1865, just as the period of Reconstruction was starting. Had Lincoln lived, the fate of freed slaves would have been radically different.

With Lincoln dead, Southern states stole land promised by the government to freed slaves and enacted "black codes." The codes kept freed slaves in the positions of farmer and servant, restricted their right to own property and limited their right of movement. Children were forced into apprenticeships for whites. Local authorities and white supremacy groups like the Ku Klux Klan enforced the codes with violence and terror.

Northerners objected to President Johnson's handling of Reconstruction and the "black codes." Congress eventually took control of Reconstruction and forced Southern states to adopt the Civil War Amendments and 1866 Civil Rights Act (over Johnson's presidential veto). These federal laws gave the freed slaves the right to vote, equal protection of the laws, and due process of law. The Freedmen's Bureau was created to establish banks, hospitals, schools and universities in the South.

For the next few years, freed slaves made tremendous progress. The Freedmen's Bureau built 3,000 schools, including Howard University and Fisk University. Freed slaves were politically active. During Reconstruction sixteen black Americans were elected to Congress, and over six hundred were elected to state legislatures and local offices. Federal troops and Freedmen's Bureau representatives were on the ground in the South to enforce protections for freed slaves.

Freed slaves outnumbered whites, and this reality caused fear and alarm in Southern whites. As long as the federal government was directly involved in Reconstruction, freed slaves had a chance at the equality and integration society promised them. But this did not last long. The Freedmen's Bureau was shut down in 1872, and in 1877 federal troops were withdrawn from the South. An economic depression hit America in 1874. Congress and the North lost interest in the cause of the freed slaves. Southern states were free to reestablish white supremacy without interference from the federal government.

As a result, blacks in the South were denied voting rights and segregated in all aspects of society (schools, health care, transportation, hotels, restaurants). Freed slaves never received their deposits back when Congress closed the Freedmen's Bank in 1874. Those who challenged white supremacy in its many forms were lynched, burned, shot or suffered other means of terror and intimidation. Homes and churches were burned. Volunteers from the North were murdered.

This was the era known as "Jim Crow." It lasted for one hundred years, until the Civil Rights Movement of the 1960s. One hundred years of oppression, terror and inequality, followed by a bloody resistance to the Civil Rights Movement. How can we say this recent history has no effect on today?

What about freed slaves who left the South?

Freed slaves left for the industrialized cities of the North during the Great Migration. At the end of the Civil War, 90% of the black population in America lived in the South. By the 1970's, this percentage was less than half. By 1920, the black population in Philadelphia had increased by 500%, and in Detroit the increase was 600%. This massive increase led to competition for jobs and housing, especially after troops returned from World War I in 1918.

Housing segregation and discrimination kept blacks in the least desirable parts of the city. One exception was Harlem, where black artists, musicians, writers, intellectuals and leaders flourished during the age of the Harlem Renaissance.

Tensions in the cities led to race riots, and the summer of 1919 was called the "Red Summer." White gangs burned black homes, and the city government created new laws preventing blacks from owning or rebuilding on burned land. As a result, thousands of black families were left homeless by the riots. The president at the time, Woodrow Wilson, publicly blamed whites for starting the race riots in Washington, DC and Chicago.

Black wealth was also destroyed in the race riots. In the Tulsa Race Riot of 1921, airplanes dropped bombs on "Black Wall Street" - the predominantly black town of Greenwood in Tulsa, Oklahoma. Greenwood was an extremely prosperous town, home to black-owned businesses, black professionals, entrepreneurs and black multi-millionaires. White mobs burned Greenwood down and murdered Greenwood residents. Some blacks tried to defend the town and its wealth, but they were outnumbered.

Did the presidency of Barrack Obama end racism?

The election of Barrack Obama led some to believe that America's racial wounds had been healed. There was talk of America becoming a colorblind or "post-race" society. Some Indian immigrants point to the election of Barrack Obama as proof that race is no longer a barrier to success in America.

The election of Barrack Obama means that a majority of

Americans gave him a chance, and he made the most of that chance. That is progress.

However, just because there are famous, successful black people doesn't mean we live in a colorblind society. Likewise, just because there are successful women does not mean sexism does not exist. Many factors affect whether people succeed. We should not be so blind to deny that race is still a factor for some.

A colorblind society doesn't happen because a black man is elected president. It will take an honest understanding of history, smart policies, dedicated people with open minds and open hearts, and time.

Are you saying Americans are racist?

No. I think most Americans are tragically uninformed about America's racial history and because of our systems of power, these uninformed Americans are often the ones creating policy and cultural norms based on stereotypes and ignorance.

Blackface is a good example. American journalist Megyn Kelly was called a racist for defending blackface on Halloween. She said that in her neighborhood growing up, this was OK.

Kelly was incredibly uninformed about America's racial history. Somehow she got through college and law school, as well as a career in journalism, and never learned why blackface is offensive to black people. This is not only a failure on Kelly's part, but also our education system. The fact that she rose to such a prominent position without this knowledge also reveals what our society values. I don't know if she is a racist, but she is ignorant. What we should be asking is why our society is producing such ignorant adults, and why we pay them millions to spread their ignorance.

What is white flight?

The phrase "white flight" refers to whites moving from an area in large numbers around the same time. The phrase became popular after World War II, when whites moved from urban areas to suburbs. Race and economics plays a role in white flight. The suburbs represented "the good life" - an escape from the over-crowded city, a chance at a single family home and plot of land, less crime and pollution and free, quality public schools. Lower levels of poverty in the suburbs meant taxes could be spent on services like parks, libraries and schools.

But the good life was not available to blacks. Real estate agents, banks and intimidation kept blacks from the suburbs. Even blacks who could afford to move were kept out. This was not the case with European and Asian immigrants, who were welcome in the new suburbs if they could afford it. Whites leaving the city were heading to all-white suburbs. Depending on the area and the family, this could be a reason for the departure.

After the Fair Housing Act of 1968, the discriminatory practices of realtors and banks were forbidden by law, and blacks attempted to move out of the city. A new form of white flight emerged, this one within the suburbs. I grew up in the 1980's, and even then it was common to hear warnings that "selling to blacks" meant prop-erty values for the town would drop. My grandparents, both immi-grants, spoke about this a lot with their immigrant friends. I'd challenge them on this as a kid, and they'd respond that they'd love to sell to blacks, but they couldn't do that to their neighbors.

What is white privilege?

America is a white majority country and whites have always been the racial group in power, so it is not surprising that being white does brings privileges in terms of access to power and resources. This is true of white majority countries, just as I would be at a disadvantage if I lived in a non-white country, such as India.

Other aspects of white privilege are more subtle. One in partic-ular is the privilege of being seen as an individual, not a reflection of your racial group. People in the majority race may rely on racial stereotypes, so the actions of non-whites are then viewed against the backdrop of that stereotype. For example, you see a black thief on television, and the next time you are in a store you are nervous the black shopper next to you is a thief. You do not stop to consider that the thief on television does not represent the majority of blacks. The same would be true if I said something unintelligent in India - some Indians would presume all American white women are unintelligent.

For most of us, this is unintentional and basic human nature. What we see is what we know, and if we don't see different types of black people, we presume that what we see is the whole picture. If this picture confirms existing stereotypes, then those stereotypes just get stronger.

However - and this is the critical point - some people in the majority will use these unintentional tendencies of human nature to hold onto power and deny opportunities to minorities. They use stereotypes to divide, and it usually works, especially on those insecure about their position in the majority class. Southern politicians learned this lesson when they used race to divide poor whites and freed slaves after the Civil War. Poor Southerners of both races would have been in a better position if they had united against white landowners. Whites in power knew this, and convinced poor whites to chose sides based on race, not economic interests.

Why don't white people like to talk about white privilege?

Well, one thing you may have learned from this book is that many Americans reject the idea of privilege in any form. From a young age, they are taught that America is the land of equality. They want to believe that they earned what they have on their own, and that they deserve it. This is firmly rooted in the American identity. Privilege is a difficult word for Americans. Many whites can't see beyond the word "privilege" to understand what those exposing white privilege are trying to say.

Accepting that there are conditions that might make it easier for a white person than a black person to succeed in America does not diminish the hard work and struggles of white Americans, or make their success any less earned. It takes a whole lot more than white privilege for whites to be successful. White privilege doesn't deny that

whites have their own struggles, too. Just because you may have benefitted from white privilege doesn't mean you thought it was right. The
average person doesn't have the means or ability to change a system
built over hundreds of years, even if they know there is a problem.

Some white people deny white privilege exists as a defensive
move - they feel they are being blamed for conditions they did not
create. White privilege is not the "fault" of most white people - fault
belongs to the whites who create the systems of privilege, intentionally keep others out and pretend there is no privilege at all. Worse,
these whites turn the question of privilege around and point to the
privileges given to blacks, with affirmative action at the top of the
list. They ask why we are even talking about white privilege, if the
goal is a colorblind society.

Yes, a colorblind society is a worthy goal, but even the brief
summary of American history included in this chapter makes clear
that we aren't there yet. Reversing the course of history is not easy,
and we shouldn't act like it is.

Actually, it seems like a lot of Americans don't like to talk about race at all.

This is true, but not for the reason you might think. It isn't about
racism or white privilege. A lot of white people feel bad about how
America has treated blacks, but don't know how to express it. They
feel uncomfortable, so they would rather avoid the topic.

I recommended that my mother read Michelle Obama's autobi-
ography, *Becoming*. I could tell she was uncomfortable reading it, as
many white Americans are uncomfortable learning about the struggles of African-Americans. The reason for her discomfort was a
surprise for me. I thought perhaps she was like her parents, who
didn't want to hear complaints about America. Perhaps she thought
Mrs. Obama didn't have a right to complain - after all, her life
turned out pretty good! Maybe she didn't want Mrs. Obama ruining
her vision of America?

No, it wasn't any of that. "I feel bad," my mom said. "I feel bad that she had to go through that." She felt bad, and didn't know what to do with those feelings. My mom couldn't fix the South Side of Chicago (Mrs. Obama's home town), or change the way others view a powerful black woman. Those problems seem overwhelming. "Feeling bad" causes many Americans to shut down when it comes to discussing race.

I recently heard a historian put this question to descendants of white slave owners, "How does it feel to inherit the legacy of slavery?" She honestly wanted to know, without judgment, without blame. She said we need to get beyond the guilt and shame on both sides of the racial divide to honestly address the legacy of slavery and Jim Crow.

I sat in the audience thinking about her question for a long time. My ancestors weren't slave owners, and arrived in this country long after the Civil War. Still, they benefitted from slavery - every American did. Slave labor built this country.

My stomach didn't feel good. I didn't feel good, and that was the answer to her question. It doesn't feel good as a white person to inherit the legacy of slavery, it doesn't feel good at all. That is one reason why many whites do not want to talk about race.

What is white supremacy?

White supremacy is the belief that whites are superior to other races. It is not the same as white privilege. In fact, many white supremacists deny the existence of white privilege. They point to differences in income and education levels as evidence of white superiority, unrelated to conditions in society that benefit whites.

White supremacists are extremists in American culture - both political parties denounce white supremacists and white supremacy groups such as Neo-Nazis and the Ku Klux Klan. There is great concern in America that President Trump is allied with white supremacist groups.

. . .

Is America's racial past just an excuse for inequalities in America?

For some, the wage and education gap is a direct result of slavery and Jim Crow. Others say those obstacles are in the past, and point to legal changes and successful blacks in the middle and upper class as evidence. As President Obama often says when asked about race in America today, "Things are better. They may not be where we need them to be, but they are better."

A friend of mine who is a descendant of slaves explained how she makes peace with America's racial past. She has seen the effects of slavery and injustice in her family and her community.

"It ends with me," she told me. She is a thriving, successful young woman, despite the history of her family.

That is the ideal for all of us, I suppose. Understanding the past, but not letting it determine the future.

15

EDUCATION - PRE-K THROUGH HIGH SCHOOL

"What is his position in the class?"

This is the question an Indian mother asked her son's school counselor some years ago.

"Don't worry, he is a good student," replied the counselor.

"I'm not worried," the mother said. "I just want to know his rank."

The counselor never told her. He probably misunderstood the mother's question and saw her as an overly competitive Indian parent pushing her kid too hard.

What the counselor didn't know is that in India class rank is the main indicator of student performance. It's how you can tell "how he's doing." In an overpopulated country like India, opportunity only goes to the highest achievers - those at the top of the class. Doing your best isn't enough. You have to be better than your peers.

Americans make the mistake of misreading this mother's competition as crass, offensive and harmful. The American view of achievement - just do your personal best - comes from a privileged, first world perspective. You can be satisfied with your personal best if you know there is enough opportunity for everyone, if you know that in the end things will work out fine. What Americans don't realize is how untrue that is for most places in the world, including India.

Indians as a group are more educated than the average American. Seventy-two percent of Indians have a bachelors degree or higher, compared with thirty percent of Americans. Still, Indian parents tell me that the differences between education in India and America make it difficult for them to be as involved in their children's education as they would like. Hopefully, this chapter can help.

Is education mandatory in the U.S.?

Yes. Education is mandatory and parents who do not send their children to school commit a minor crime called "truancy." The definition and punishment for truancy varies by state, as is the case with much about education in America.

Are schools free?

It is true that a free, public education is available to every child in America. Students in public school don't pay for books, transportation or uniforms. Parents pay for school supplies at the start of the school year and school trips.

What are the different levels of education before college?

Public school begins in Kindergarten, when a child is five or six years old (depending on the town cut-off date). Most school districts do not offer free education before Kindergarten, so parents pay for private Pre-Kindergarten (Pre-K) programs starting as early as two years old. Elementary school is from Kindergarten through fifth or sixth grade, then students attend Middle School for two or three years, and finally High School (also known as Secondary School) until the final year, twelfth grade.

Are there board exams in tenth grade?

No, the U.S. does not have a system of board exams like India.

Students do not select an academic field of study until they declare a "major" in college, usually in their second year. Before that, the focus is on a broad range of subjects, not specialized or career focused. Students study foreign languages, art, music, civics, health and other topics in addition to the core subjects. Most colleges also have required courses that force students to broaden their education beyond their major.

What are my options for school?

Almost every town has a local public school. In cities, schools pull from the local area, unless the state allows for "school choice," which we will discuss later. In some areas, students can take a test for a specialized high school. These are also free and focus on certain disciplines such as science, the arts and public service.

Parents can pay to send their children to private schools. Private schools are independent or religious. Charter schools are public schools organized by a group, often to teach with a particular theme or philosophy. Trade schools (also called vocational schools) teach job skills and are run by the public school system. There are also some children home schooled in America for a variety of reasons. This is regulated by the state and parents must comply with requirements for the home schooling to be accepted as a substitute for public or private education.

Is there a difference in education quality from state to state?

Yes, and even from town to town. Most of the funds for American public education come from local property taxes. This is why towns with the highest property taxes usually have the strongest school districts. As for regional differences, strong schools can be found everywhere, but in general the schools near metropolitan areas are strongest.

. . .

Do children live away at school in America?

Boarding schools, also known as "prep schools," do exist in the U.S., but they are not common. They are seen as reserved for the elite, even though many offer generous scholarships. These boarding schools start in ninth grade - it is extremely rare for an elementary age child to be sent away to school.

What is school choice?

In "school choice" states students can apply to attend other public schools outside of their neighborhood. Florida is a state with school choice.

What is the school schedule in the U.S.?

In the Northeast, school generally begins in early September and ends in late June. In Western and Southern states, the school year begins in August and ends in May. School generally ends at 3 pm.

What is aftercare?

Now that most women work outside the home, schools provide after school care for a fee, usually until 5:30 or 6 pm. Some schools even offer before care for parents who must be at work before school begins.

What is the Pledge of Allegiance?

It may not seem very "American" to force school children to recite an oath of allegiance to their country at the start of each school day. That is why the Pledge of Allegiance has been contro-versial since its adoption.

The original Pledge came about in the 1880's, largely due to fears over the arrival of millions of European immigrants. Native born Americans felt something had to be done to prove loyalty to the U.S. and guard against the loss of a true American identity. The Pledge was not officially adopted by Congress until 1942, a time of national anxiety over communism, fascism and World War II. In an effort to distinguish the U.S. from communist states, the phrase "under God" was added to the Pledge in 1954.

There's a lot to challenge here, and the Pledge kept the U.S. Supreme Court busy for years. In 1940, the Supreme Court ruled that public schools could mandate the Pledge after it was challenged by a Jehovah's witness. Then, in 1943, the Supreme Court reversed its earlier decision in the case *West Virginia State Board of Education v. Barnette.* Justice Robert Jackson wrote the following eloquent condemnation of forced loyalty pledges:

"If there is any fixed star in our constitutional constellation, it is that no official, high or petty, can prescribe what shall be orthodox in politics, nationalism, religion, or other matters of opinion, or force citizens to confess by word or act their faith therein."[1]

The parents of Jehovah's Witness school children objected to the Pledge because under their religion saluting the flag or reciting the Pledge is an act of worship, and worship is reserved for God alone.

While the federal government cannot mandate school children recite the Pledge, states can. In fact, most states do have this requirement, although local schools generally follow their own rules.

The Supreme Court has not directly ruled on whether the "under God" phrase violates the First Amendment. However, the Supreme Court has stated that "under God" is not a religious claim.

So, if you or your child is required by state or local law to recite the Pledge of Allegiance and you have no objection that would be protected under the Constitution, the safest thing to do is place your right hand over your heart and say the Pledge.

What should I expect from American teachers?

Teachers in America are not as respected as they are in India. Since my father was a teacher, this has always bothered me. There is even a popular saying in America, "Those who can, do. Those who can't, teach." This is very insulting to all teachers.

Of course, there are bad teachers just like in any profession. My father complained about them and even discouraged me from becoming a teacher because he thought I'd be frustrated by colleagues who were only there for the benefits (state workers receive generous health benefits and pensions) and the vacations (summers off, long breaks during the year). Also, teachers with "tenure" cannot be fired, so bad ones hang around for too long.

Americans don't give out respect easily. They believe respect should be earned. So a good teacher will be respected, but it is not the case that teachers will be universally respected because they are teachers.

Don't be afraid to talk to you child's teachers. This is not disrespectful, and should not affect how the teacher treats your child.

How do I make sure my child is challenged academically?

Unfortunately, in many elementary schools advanced students are not challenged. Parents will enroll bright students in enrichment programs outside of school, perhaps at a local university, library, museum or a franchise like Kumon or JEI. There are also countless online options for enrichment and advanced study that are cheaper (some free) and more convenient. An Indian friend gets grammar and math books from India because she does not think the American elementary schools teach these subjects well.

Until middle school, most kids are on the same "track." Some schools have "gifted" programs based on IQ scores, but for the most part all students learn at the same pace. In middle school and high school students can be in the "honors" track, which is more challenging.

Are children permitted to write with the left hand?

Yes. Schools do not take a position on this. Some schools have stopped teaching script (cursive) and spend more time on typing.

What is the role of technology in the classroom?

Many schools are using laptops in class, and even give laptops (usually Chrome books) to each student. There is a debate over the value of educational technology. Parents seeking to limit "screen" time may not want their children staring at screens at school and for homework. As you can imagine, it is big business as well, and educational technology companies are selling to schools that fear they will be left behind in the digital age.

Ironically, some schools take the opposite approach and keep technology out of the classroom. Some of these schools are even in Silicon Valley, the heart of the digital world.

Cell phones are often allowed in school, but can only be used during lunch. This is hard for schools to enforce, and teachers find themselves competing with cell phones for the attention of students in class.

What is a public library?

Benjamin Franklin began the free public library system in the U.S., and Andrew Carnegie expanded it to become a reality. Every town has a free public library where residents can borrow books, videos, magazines and other media, and attend library events. It is a quiet place for studying (and writing!). Most libraries have a section dedicated to children's books. I highly recommend using your local library.

American children and reading

One older female Indian immigrant told me she was scolded as a young girl in India for reading story books. Her mother said it was silly to read stories when she should be studying. I suspect today parents would be happy to see their kid's head in a book instead of in front of a screen.

Reading is a highly valued skill and popular hobby in America. Schools encourage parents to help children develop a "love" of reading by reading with them and requiring at least thirty minutes of reading each night. While many Indian parents in America say they were not read to as a child, they do read to their children.

What is a "weighted average"?

One Indian mom told me she discouraged her son from taking the most advanced classes in high school because she thought he would get higher grades in the easier courses. When he graduated, she realized that the students in the advanced classes had "weighted" grade point averages (GPA), meaning they received extra points just for being in the more difficult class. Her son did not get these points, and as a result had a lower GPA and rank than the others. She wishes she had known about the "weighted" average before selecting classes for her son.

What if my kid is bullied?

Bullying is taken very seriously by schools, at least that is what they say. School officials and teachers want to know about bullying, but the response varies based on the school. What makes bullying difficult is that it often happens when the teacher is not around, so schools cannot verify what happened. School officials are political, and fear the reaction of a child falsely accused. Still, you should always make the school aware of any bullying in writing. Keep a copy of the letter or email as proof.

Kids often do not talk about being bullied. Pay attention to changes you notice in your child and maintain open communication with teachers. Schools have counselors and therapists who can help.

Indians who grow up in the U.S. may get bullied because of their skin color or name. One parent said children have to develop a thick skin so they can survive. After all, we will encounter bullies at every stage of life, and cannot be offended easily or they will win.

One immigrant told me about a boy who touched her shoulder while she sat eating in the school cafeteria. He did it again, and again. Finally, she stood up and slapped him across the face. She ran to the principal's office, worried about what her parents would think. She feared she had disappointed them and wasted their hard work to bring her to this country. As it turns out, the boy was a trouble maker and suspended from school because of his actions.

When this happened, she was new to America and didn't know the customs. Still, she felt it was wrong of him to touch her so deliberately and repeatedly without permission. She trusted her instincts and knew it didn't feel right. You can say she trusted her "gut" as it might be called in America. The boy should not have touched her, and the principal recognized this. She didn't get in trouble at school or home that day, and she would not forget the lesson she learned - to trust her gut and stand up for herself.

She teaches the same lesson to her kids. When she noticed her son was shy and did not speak up when other kids took his toys or pushed him around, she enrolled him in martial arts. This is a popular hobby for American children of both genders. Martial arts gave him confidence to defend himself, as she had done that day in the cafeteria.

What if my kid is a bully?

Realize that what may be acceptable in India or when you were growing up may be considered bullying today. Our understanding of what is acceptable is always changing, but if we don't pay attention, our kids can end up behaving in ways that have serious consequences.

My advice is to find out what happened, talk to your kid so that they understand why the behavior is unacceptable, enforce consequences and - schools do not like this - talk to the parent of the bullied child. This is so critically important. Usually schools will not even tell you who the child is, but your kid will. This clears up any misunderstandings and can promote healing on both sides. You may even want to invite them over. Set the example for your child to follow.

A word on violence

Your kid will be entering school at a time when school shootings have made any talk of death or killing a cause for alarm. Even though video games and movies for kids are extremely violent, kids must know not to play or speak violently in school or they will be seen as a threat. This is confusing for kids, and takes careful explaining by parents.

What are AP courses?

"Advanced Placement" or "AP" courses are college level courses offered in high school. Some colleges give college credit for these courses if the student scores well on the AP test. This allows students to skip introductory college classes and possibly graduate early.

What are "special needs" and "special education"?

If a teacher recommends that your child be "evaluated" for special education services, do not be alarmed or afraid. The term "special education" includes a broad list of services, such speech therapy, occupational therapy, academic assistance and counseling. Children can receive services for as long or as short as they need them, and many children do. The services are provided free by the school for children with qualifying conditions.

Parents may be concerned that special education is a negative label that can limit a child. This may have been the case years ago, but a lot has changed in special education. Even the use of the name "special needs" instead of "retarded" shows a new understanding and acceptance of the different ways students learn. The rise of ADHD and autism in school-age children has made "special needs" common and familiar.

The school cannot provide services without your consent. Advocates can help guide you through the process. Parents who are informed and involved in the process usually get what their kids need. As is true with education in general, some school districts are more supportive than others. It is even more important to pick the right school district when you have a special needs child.

What is Common Core?

Forty-two states have adopted the Common Core State Standards Initiative as goals and guides for the teaching of math and English from kindergarten to twelfth grade. It is not a federal program, and participation is not mandatory. As parents, you may find that the new teaching methods make it harder to help your children with homework. This depends on where you were educated, though. Some immigrants, in particular from Europe, have said the Common Core methods are actually similar to what they learned in school.

What does "well rounded student" mean?

It is not a polite term for fat. This means the student is strong in a variety of disciplines, both academic and non-academic. A good student in America is a "well rounded" student. The laser focus on one subject you may find in other countries is not rewarded in the U.S.

Are students ranked?

Not until twelfth grade, and it is not public.

Unlike in India, there is little focus on class rank in America. A student's rank does not help much with college admissions because it varies based on the strength of the high school. The "valedictorian" is the student at the top of the class, and "salutatorian" is the student in second place. Both usually speak at graduation.

What is the Honor Roll?

Each school sets a GPA cutoff for the quarterly "honor roll." The National Honor Society is a national society based on grade point average, teacher recommendation and community service. There is a National Honor Society for middle school and high school.

Will the high school help us with college admission?

Some high schools have college counselors on staff, or even whole departments. Others leave it to the parents to find resources online. Deadlines are important in the college admissions process, not just for applications, but for financial aid as well. College planning starts the first year of high school. Talk to your child's "Guidance Counselor" and read up on the process. Don't rely on your kid. Teachers aren't involved beyond writing recommendations for students. Other parents might be helpful, especially if they went through the process recently.

College admission becomes an obsession for too many American parents. It is not enough to go to college, but their kids must go to the "right" college.

What is hot lunch?

Hot lunch is the food served in the school cafeteria. Students pay for these meals. Students can bring food from home if they do not want hot lunch.

In the past few years, schools have recognized the importance of serving healthier meals in schools. Michelle Obama made this a priority when she was First Lady. Soda is no longer available in most schools.

. . .

What is a lunch lady/lunch monitor?

The toughest job in the school, in my opinion. The lunch lady is responsible for keeping order in the lunch room and on the play ground. I would not take this job if it paid a million dollars. If you have school age children, you understand why.

Why do some kids get free lunch?

The National Free Lunch Program is run by the U.S. Department of Agriculture. The program subsidizes the cost of school lunch for those who qualify (low income families).

The number of students receiving free lunch is public information, and some use these figures to determine the poverty level in a school.

16

EDUCATION - THE COLLEGE
ADMISSIONS PROCESS

Beware visa mills and "pay to stay" scams.

As I write this, the U.S. government is cracking down on "visa mills" - schools that exist for the sole reason of giving foreign students a way to remain in the country on a student visa. In the most recent case, the University of Farmington in Michigan was set up as a fake school by the government to catch immigration fraud. ICE raided the homes of recruiters, school officials and students, arrested more than one hundred students and sent them to detention centers. Some of the students paid $20,000 to attend the fake school.

How can you protect yourself? Don't be convinced by a website. You are going to have to talk to people at the school. Ask to speak with current students, recent graduates and professors. Confirm that the college is a legitimate, accredited institution. Often the visa mill schools go to India to recruit students. Beware of these recruiters. If you suspect the school is fake, don't take the risk.

Does it really matter which college you attend?

It depends on the industry. In more traditional industries that have not yet been disrupted by technology, college prestige still matters. Someone explained to me that if you graduate from a well known school, employers assume you are smart enough to learn what they need to teach you. Here's the catch - employers no longer have the time or resources to teach new hires. You have to come in the door with skills, not a prestigious diploma.

In the technology field, employers want to know what you can do, not where you went to school. Too many Americans waste their college years and think they can rely on their college name to get a job. As a result, they don't have the skills employers want. Who has them? Immigrants.

Many immigrants from China and India attend schools unknown to most Americans - either in their home country or on American soil. Community colleges, technical schools, lesser known public universities - immigrants make the most of whatever school they are at. Their work ethic and drive are what employers want.

Companies complain that students are graduating from elite colleges without job skills or work experience. Professors at famous schools often spend more time on research and speaking than in the classroom, leaving the teaching to graduate students. Students from less prestigious schools, many of whom work during college and have close relationships with professors, are landing the jobs of the future.

Consider this - everyone knows about Stanford, but this school accepts less than 5% of applicants. Employers know that if they only hire from Stanford, they are missing out on a lot of talent.

What are the college "rankings"?

What you need to know is that the college rankings are not scientific - they are highly subjective and can be manipulated by colleges. The most well known rankings are from the now defunct magazine U.S. News & World Report. It is remarkable that after decades of publication, this publication could not continue as a magazine, but sales of the rankings were so strong that they continued the annual edition. The rankings are not impartial - they are compiled for a profit. They may be a rough guide at best, but really don't mean anything about the quality of a school.

What is affirmative action?

Affirmative action is similar to the Indian policy of "reservation" - almost. Reservation is a better name because it is honest about the goal - to reserve seats for underrepresented minorities. Affirmation action is a vague term that Americans often misunderstand and, at least to some white Americans, seems unfair.

In 2016, the Supreme Court ruled that considering a student's race in college admissions as one of many factors does not violate the Constitution. This is known as "race-conscious admissions" and is different than quotas, which are not permitted. If the ordinary application process cannot yield a diverse class, the college may then consider race as a factor.

Is it harder for Asian-American students to be accepted at elite colleges?

Yes.

Why?

In 2018, a group representing Asian-American students sued Harvard for discrimination. The case is *Students for Fair Admissions v. Harvard*, and the lawsuit is in a Boston federal court. The litigation documents reveal how Harvard makes admission decisions, and it will shock you.

Harvard uses three categories - academic, personal and extra-curricular. Of the three, the personal category is considered most important and the academic category the least important.[1] Yes, you read that right. Colleges like Harvard will argue that this is because all of their applicants are academically qualified, but there is a difference between academically qualified and academically excellent. You would think Harvard would only want students who excel, and make that the top priority in admission, but that is not the case.

Why? Well, for one thing, money matters. Less qualified applicants with connections to donors are given preference. College athletes bring in money for the college, so less qualified athletes are also given a preference - a huge preference. Recruited athletes with mediocre academic ratings were accepted at a rate of 70%, while other students with the same academic rating were accepted at a rate of .076% (Karabel outlines this in his article). Legacies are also given a significant benefit in admissions (discussed below).

The case against Harvard isn't about donors, athletes or legacies, although it should be if anyone is seriously interested in fairness in college admissions. Donors, athletes and legacies are protected groups with deep, institutional, influential roots at Harvard. Their privilege in the admissions game is unquestioned, almost sacred.

In the case, Students for Fair Admissions ask why overqualified Asian-Americans with exceptional grades, test scores and extra-curriculars are rejected from Harvard when others who appear less qualified are accepted. They claim there is a higher standard for Asian-American students, supported by disparities in test scores like the SAT and ACT (the average Asian-American score is more than 100 points higher than other groups admitted) and that Harvard penalized Asian-American students to achieve predetermined racial percentages in the student body.

So what excuse does Harvard give for rejecting so many overqualified Asian-American students? According to the Harvard admission documents, Asian-Americans do not score as high as their peers in the "personal qualities" category. Using a vague, personality-based category to keep out overqualified applicants is the same strategy Harvard used in the twentieth century to keep the number of admitted Jews to 15% or lower. The history of Harvard's intentional discrimination against Jews is set forth in the complaint filed by Students for Fair Admissions. In the 1920's and 1930's, Harvard saw

Jews as disrupting the campus culture long dominated by wealthy white Protestants. Today, Harvard appears to see Asian-American students as a similar threat, perhaps to the wealthy white alumni with children less qualified than Asian-Americans. Regardless of the outcome, the case is likely to be appealed to the U.S. Supreme Court.

I have to note that the group bringing the lawsuit, Students for Fair Admissions, is not supported by many Asian-Americans. In 2013 the same lawyer in the Harvard case brought a lawsuit against the University of Texas at Austin alleging discrimination against a white student, and lost. Some feel the lawyer is using Asian-Americans in his broader fight against affirmative action.

What is a legacy?

I have spoken a lot in this book about Americans loving the story of the "self made man/woman." It doesn't matter where you come from in America - wealth and class are not determined by birth like they are in other countries. Well, legacies are an exception to this and in my opinion, very un-American.

A legacy is the child of an alumnus (parent who graduated from the school). Legacies are given preference in admissions. For example, the lawsuit against Harvard revealed that about 15% of the entering freshman class were legacies - one in eleven students. It is a big number for a category immigrants and lower class Americans can't compete in.

Some leading institutions do not give any preference to children of alumni: Oxford, Cambridge, MIT, California Institute of Technology (CalTech) and University of California at Berkeley. Hopefully others will soon follow them.

Are there any colleges where Asian-American students have better chances of acceptance?

Some schools do not consider race or ethnicity in admissions, and you will usually see higher percentages of Asian-Americans at these schools. Two examples are CalTech and University of California at Berkeley, where Asian-Americans are at or above 40%.

How can Asian-Americans increase their chances of college admission?

The answer is to not limit yourself to only a few schools that everyone knows. America is overflowing with universities - you don't have to go to the most famous or most expensive. Focus on what you want to do in college, not where you go. Do well in college, and you will be successful afterwards. One thing I hope we all can learn from the Harvard lawsuit is that a Harvard degree doesn't mean as much as we thought it did.

If you aren't convinced, well, you can pay a college consultant who specializes in Asian-American admissions to tell you how to beat the quotas. Or you can change your name and lie on your application, although I strongly recommend against doing that.

What is a liberal arts college?

Liberal arts colleges focus on a broad education, often more theoretical than practical, and not pre-professional. Their goal is to teach students "how to think." The art history major who applied to medical school probably came from a liberal arts school. Liberal arts schools have course requirements such as foreign language, writing and small-class seminars.

You might be surprised to learn that most of the well known American colleges are liberal arts colleges. At my college, for example, students couldn't take a business course - they had to take economics. Students could not take accounting. My husband, an accountant, was a math major. Even the Education Department was viewed as too pre-professional.

What is a community college?

Community colleges offer classes that can usually be transferred when a student switches to a four year college. The maximum degree offered by a community college is a two year degree, or an "Associate's Degree." Tuition is not expensive, and admission is easy. You may find adults at community college acquiring new skills. Most do not offer on-campus housing so students live at home and commute to school. Since college is so expensive, some families feel a year or two at community college can help a student mature and focus before entering college.

What is the Ivy League?

The Ivy League is known as a group of eight elite colleges, but it was originally created for the purpose of college athletics (the teams in the Ivy League play each other). These colleges are all located in the Northeast and are some of the oldest in the country. The Ivy League schools are: Harvard, Princeton, Yale, University of Pennsylvania, Cornell, Dartmouth, Brown and Columbia.

The schools in the Ivy League are so different from each other that the title is really meaningless, despite what you may think. It is a remnant from colonial times - don't let your concept of a good school be stuck in the past.

What is a state school?

These are schools in the state system, meaning they are funded and run by the state in which the school is located. The New York state school system is "SUNY" (State University of New York), and the California state schools are known as the "UC" system. Students who reside in the state pay lower tuition at state schools than students who live in other states. This is called "in-state tuition" and is often half of the tuition price for out of state students.

What is an HBCU?

This stands for "Historically Black Colleges and Universities." Student of any race can attend an HBCU, although the main mission of the school is to educate black Americans. Howard University, Moorehouse College and Spelman College are the most well known HBCUs. Presidential candidate Kamala Harris, who is of Indian and Jamaican ancestry, graduated from Howard University.

17

EDUCATION - THE COLLEGE YEARS

In America, way too much focus is put on the college admissions process, and not what students plan to do in college. Students arrive at college "burned out" from working so hard to get into college that they too often don't take college as seriously as high school. It sounds ridiculous, but it happens.

The "country club" atmosphere at many private colleges distracts students from the reality of preparing for a career. It's not just the students, though. Many college professors and administrators do not think as much as they should about helping students find jobs after college.

How expensive is college in the U.S.?

In 2018, the average tuition for one year at a private, four year college was about $35,000. For a public (state) school the average was approximately $10,000 (in-state) and $20,000 (out-of-state).

American colleges are the most expensive in the world - some private schools charge $70,000 a year for tuition, room and board (dorm room and food). You can understand why many parents start saving for college when their children are born.

For the sake of comparison, Oxford University in England, a public school, costs less than $15,000 a year for U.S. students.

Are international students eligible for financial aid?

Most international students studying on the undergraduate level in the U.S. pay full tuition (about 80%). Federal financial aid is only available to U.S. citizens, with few exceptions (for example, people in the U.S. seeking asylum). You may receive a scholarship directly from the college you are attending, but these are competitive for international students.

Can I work if I am on a student visa?

If you are on an F-1 visa, you can work only on campus for the first year of study, and after that you can work off campus if it is approved by the university and related to your course of study.

While your parents may be paying tuition for the American university, you will soon learn that you need to work to cover living expenses in the U.S. An Indian immigrant on a student visa told me that as soon as he got his Social Security number he knocked on every professor's door asking for work. Unlike the American students, he didn't have a car or much spending money. Campus jobs don't pay a lot, and there could be limits on the hours you work. Still, at least for the first year, this will be your only option if you are in the U.S. on a student visa.

What types of financial aid are available to U.S. students?

Financial aid in the U.S. is complicated. It begins with a family completing the FAFSA form ("Federal Application for Free Student Aid"). The information submitted about your income and assets will be used to compute your EFC - "Expected Family Contribution." The formula used for this computation is set by federal law. If the cost of a college is above your EFC, you are entitled to need based federal aid to make up the difference. This does not mean you have to pay the entire EFC, or that you will get aid to cover the difference between the EFC and the cost of college.

The federal government offers several forms of need-based financial aid, including grants, subsidized loans (the government pays the interest while the student is in college) and work-study programs. Students can also apply for merit scholarships either from the school or other sources. Colleges may also offer tuition reductions as incentives for athletes or other in-demand students to attend. Families can also consider non-need based aid, including unsubsidized federal loans.

Should I take out private loans if federal loans and scholarships are not enough?

Advisors recommend using federal loans first, since they usually have a lower interest rate than private loans. I used private loans for graduate school. I am still paying off these loans each month. I read that Barrack Obama paid off his student loans while in the White House.

Education is an investment, so I don't mind carrying the debt. That said, I do not think I was smart about my investment. The schools I went to were too expensive, and if I wasn't married to a supportive husband, there is no way I could have stopped working as a lawyer to pursue a career as a writer. The decision to take loans depends on your career and life plans.

Can I ask for more money?

Yes, and you should if you need it. Financial aid is a negotiation.

What about online colleges?

These are generally for working people who cannot physically come to campus. In most cases, they are as respected as a full-time school. They can also be very expensive. You will see online schools heavily advertised, sometimes making false promises of employment with the degree. It is more acceptable to use an online school for a certification or to increase skills, but not for a full undergraduate education.

I am on a student visa. What happens if I drop out of school?

You will lose your student visa status. If caught, you could be sent to a detention center and when you leave the country you will not be able to reenter the U.S. for up to ten years, based on how long you overstay. Currently, universities are not required to report students on student visas who withdraw from college, but this could change under the Trump Administration.

What are fraternities and sororities?

You may be wondering why Americans wear sweatshirts displaying two or three huge Greek letters. These letters refer to organizations known as fraternities and sororities. These are social groups on campus known as "Greek" life. Students "pledge" to join the groups and go through a selection process known as "rush" and "hazing." Members have to pay dues to belong. The "frat house" or "sorority house" is often a real house where members live and hold meetings and parties, although not every campus allows these. The members refer to each other as brothers/sisters.

Greek life is popular on many college campuses. Some say the organizations can be a source of networking and connections that help students later in life. These organizations have also been attacked for harsh hazing practices and excess drinking.

What is the social scene at college?

One Indian immigrant told me he was surprised to find students in the college cafeteria sat based on their race or ethnicity. The black students sat together, as did the Asians, the white students and so on. He had never experienced this self segregation at his Indian boarding school because everyone was Indian. He found it odd, and said it made it harder to make friends.

Sometimes all of the international students stick together. One Indian immigrant told me she was not accepted by the Indian international students because they came from wealthy families in New Delhi and Mumbai, and she was from a poor, rural region of India. International students pay full tuition, and many come from extremely wealthy families.

Off-campus college parties almost always have alcohol, even though the drinking age is twenty-one. These parties are often hosted by fraternities or sororities. Unfortunately, abusing alcohol is very common at college in the U.S.

Is college safe for women? What about sexual assault?

According to the Department of Justice, one in four women will be sexually assaulted during their time in college. Many of the cases involve heavy drinking and are difficult to prove. It is common for women to keep sexual assault a secret, so it is hard to know exact numbers. This is slowly changing as colleges are encouraging women to report cases and are responding in a more serious manner to the charges.

Sexual assault happens at all colleges - don't make the mistake of thinking that smart people don't commit crimes. One of the most notable sexual assault trails in recent years involved a Stanford student, and three Yale students recently sued the school for the way it handles sexual assault.

For women, my advice is this - don't ever be alone and drunk on a college campus, or anywhere else. Stay with a group, especially at parties. Be aware of your surroundings. The first thing to do after sexual assault is to call 911 (the local police). Don't rely on your college for action - get the police involved. Also, keep in mind that in the U.S., you can be assaulted or raped by a person you are dating.

For men, my advice is this - how you behave in college will affect the rest of your life. The time of partying without consequences is over. Be responsible. Respect women. In America, "no means no." No matter how far along you are, or how many times you have had sex with the person before, if you don't stop you are committing a crime. Also, sexual assault involves more than intercourse - it is any unwanted sexual contact.

Drunk and reckless students aren't the only danger on college campuses. Some of the most well known universities in the U.S. are in high crime urban areas. Schools do their best to keep the campus safe, but crime does happen. I left an elite school after a student was raped at gunpoint behind the cafeteria. It was in the middle of the afternoon. It happens everywhere, so be careful.

18

DATING & MARRIAGE

How do people meet each other in America?
Traditional arranged marriage is rare in America, but the looser version of "arranged introduction" is common. In fact, meeting through friends was the number one way couples met in 2018. The difference I have found between arranging in India and the U.S. is that in the U.S. the "matchmaker" stops at the introduction. After that, they are "hands off" - perhaps because they don't want responsibility for a bad introduction.

The next most popular way to meet is at college or work. I met my husband in college, and if I hadn't I really don't know how I would have met my match. As a lawyer, I shudder at the thought of meeting someone through work. I don't like bars and clubs, and don't trust online dating (although I know several married couples who met online). I discuss online dating below, but it seems to be fading in popularity as a way to meet a partner.

Why do Americans wait so long to get married?
I hear this question a lot. My husband and I met in college, then dated for about five more years until we got married. There is little

stigma in the U.S. for living together, or dating one person for years and marrying another.

There are practical reasons for this. Women are waiting longer to get married because they are pursuing careers. Women in my mother's generation joked that they went to college to pursue a degree in MRS - meaning to find a husband. That is no longer the case.

If I go out alone with a man, is that considered a date?

Absolutely not! It is common for unmarried men and women to be friends and do things together. Married men and women also meet together to plan events or work on projects.

Of course, if these "together" times happen when you are alone and don't involve common interests, the other person may think you are becoming more than friends. If alcohol is involved, be careful. This could be a sign the other person has sexual intentions.

What is date rape?

It is possible under law to be raped by someone you are dating, or even married to. If consent is not given, that is rape under U.S. law.

What does the term "friends with benefits" mean?

This means a friend with whom you casually hook up or have sex. This is spoken of more than actually done, but I thought you should know the phrase in case you mistake it for some other type of benefit.

What about online dating?

I have seen two types of people using online dating in America: the first are busy people who do not have time to date, the second are creeps. It can be hard to tell the difference.

. . .

So what's the deal with American women?

American women…we're a diverse bunch, but like women everywhere, we want respect. You may look at American popular culture and think American women aren't respectable. Celebrities and pop stars do not represent American women. On the whole, American women know they do not need a man for financial stability, respectability or even to have a family. This independence can be misunderstood as selfishness. However, just because a woman doesn't need a partner doesn't mean she doesn't want one. It means she can be more selective and find one that sees her as an equal.

Is gay marriage legal in the U.S.?

Yes. After years as a hot political issue, the question of gay marriage was put to rest by the 2015 Supreme Court decision in *Obergefell v. Hodges*. Before the decision, gay marriage was so divisive that even Democratic candidates would only support "civil unions" and not full marriage rights for gays.

The predictions that gay marriage would destroy the institution of marriage and morality in America were clearly false. Gay weddings are common, and gays are starting families through adoption or surrogate mothers. According to one Indian immigrant, this is not the case in India. In America, gays are accepted as part of mainstream culture. It is not news to see gays in everyday roles such as business executives, doctors, teachers and police. In India, as this immigrant shared, gays are still on the fringes of society.

When was interracial marriage legalized in the U.S.?

The 1967 Supreme Court decision in *Loving v. Virginia* (the best case name in legal history) struck down laws against interracial marriage.

. . .

Interracial dating and marriage seem very common in the U.S.

When I started dating my husband in the 1990's, my grandparents worried that our children would "be confused about who they are." They used to tell me, "Sure, it's fine for you and Nagendra to marry, but what about the children?"

Today, mixed race families are everywhere. The worries of my grandparents are unknown to the current generation, thankfully. Even when it comes up, my children speak of our different races as a matter of fact, not anything different or odd.

What is eloping?

Elope means the couple married without a wedding, and usually without telling anyone.

Is it true some couples get married in courthouses in America?

Yes, and if you go to a courthouse that performs marriages you will see many couples waiting in line. A couple could make this choice for many reasons and it is not seen as negative.

Why is divorce so common in the U.S.?

To answer this question, we need to distinguish between cases where a physical or emotional threat is present, and cases where the couple divorces for more private, personal reasons. In my experience, few Indian families understand the first reason. It is the second that is harder for them to understand.

Self fulfillment is important to Americans, and this applies to marriage. Staying together means giving up on the ideal of a fulfilling marriage. This ideal is what Americans see in our popular culture, and many get married unprepared to accept the reality. This is why you see countless books on marriage and a thriving marriage counselor business. Another reason divorce is more common today than years ago is that women are more financially independent.

There is a recognition that people who married at a young age change over time and may no longer be the best suited partners. It's also accepted that divorce can be healthier for children than growing up in a household with fighting, unhappy parents. These are some possible answers to this complicated and personal question.

19

HOME AND FAMILY LIFE

"I knew I wouldn't like America when I was on the airplane and saw a magazine picture of a woman raking leaves in a sari." An older family member told me that. The picture made her nervous. She knew her husband would be working long hours, and she would be alone to manage tasks she had never done before, like raking leaves.

Home life in America can be overwhelming. Families live alone, and domestic help is expensive. Homes require a lot of work - painting, gardening, shoveling snow, raking leaves - and that is just the outside! Professional people are still expected to manage the household, and unkept homes bring nasty comments from the neighbors.

One immigrant who worked in the IT field in New Delhi told me her work was viewed as the top priority, even over household work. A local lady cooked food for her and the other working ladies every night. She was not viewed as lazy or spoiled - it was actually the opposite. She was respected for her career and the community was there to support her. In America, you will see highly trained professionals cooking dinner, cleaning dishes and doing laundry every night.

. . .

Are men expected to cook in America?

They often must learn to cook out of necessity. One immigrant from Tamil Nadu confessed that he had never set foot in a kitchen before he came to America. He came on a student visa (master's level) and his wife was still in India, so he was living alone on a limited budget. He relied on friends to teach him to cook, and by the time his wife arrived a year later, he was a competent cook.

Are working women expected to cook meals?

My mother-in-law does not cook (she'll say she does, but that's only if she absolutely has to). I always found this unusual, since the kitchen is the place where Indian women of her generation gather. It is their kingdom. At other Indian homes, the woman of the house welcomes us with chai and a fresh, warm delicious meal. Not my mother-in-law. She will cut fruit and microwave leftovers. If we are still hungry, she'll ask if we want to order pizza. Even with such little effort, she'll still pressure us to eat. It's hysterical.

I once asked her why she doesn't cook. She was clearly insulted. "I can cook," she shot back at me.

I wanted to follow up with another question - then why don't you? - but I knew from her tone to keep quiet. I had been shamed into silence.

She gave me a reason anyway. "When I was a girl I studied," she said. "I was too busy to cook."

I almost said, "Aren't we all too busy to cook?" I was barely getting meals out for my family as a working mom at the time. The kids were eating way too much "mac & cheese" and chicken nuggets. I thought she was lucky that she could say "too busy" and get out of cooking.

My mother-in-law's situation is not shared by most Indian women coming to America today, unless you are going to be living with family who cook while you work outside the home. If not, you will be expected to work and cook dinner, and not just dinner - warm, healthy, delicious meals!

. . .

Gender Roles at Home

One Indian immigrant told me men in India just work and eat - they are not expected to be involved in the household unless there is a major decision to be made. In America, the expectations on husbands and fathers are different. They are expected to help care for the home and the children.

The generation of Indians who arrived in the 1970s and 1980s were not held to these standards. American society has changed since then, as more women work outside the home. For older Indians, it seemed that as long as the children were watched, fed and educated, not much could go wrong.

For this reason, Indian men may find themselves in unfamiliar roles after they marry and have children in America. They may be surprised that society values family time over work time. A first generation Indian married to an Indian raised outside of the U.S. shared her embarrassment when her son's teacher asked her why her son said he didn't know his father. After that, she made sure her husband spent more time with the children.

Why don't I ever see my neighbors?

Many Indian immigrants share this complaint. Americans, too, miss the days when neighbors were close and could rely on each other for help. Today, families are busy and keep to themselves. Free time is spent resting and catching up on household chores. We are shy about asking for help.

I noticed this when our neighbors asked us to "cat sit" while they were away. This meant changing the litter box and putting out new food each day. If they had not asked us, we would not have become friends. Now our families are close and it is comforting to know we have friends next door.

Housework in America

As one Indian immigrant told me, "It doesn't matter who you are in America, you still have to wash your own dishes."

In India, labor is cheap and plentiful. I remember visiting family in India and being horrified that they employed a young boy to wash dishes and clean laundry. "It is better for him to be here than on the streets," I was told. In America, only the very wealthy have live-in help, and it is generally viewed as a negative thing. If you hire a housekeeper, be prepared for Americans to act strange about it.

Another Indian immigrant shared that a wealthy friend from Mumbai decided to leave America because she would have to clean her own house. Compared to what she was expected to do in America, this woman preferred life in India. "Wives in India do nothing," she joked with me.

Why do so few Americans have household help?

Many Americans feel weird about household help, especially live-in help. My mother is very private and distrustful of outsiders - she hides her valuables whenever anyone comes to work on the house. Some worry that live-in help knows your personal business. Since most Americans did not grow up with household help, they feel awkward being "served." Slavery is a dark stain on our national past. Having someone in the house full-time could be too close to slavery for some, even if the person is being paid.

Americans will hire someone to clean their house once or twice a week, cut their lawn and babysit children, but not live in the home. When Americans do hire household help, these individuals tend to become part of the family. You do not see the class separation that I have seen in India and Indian immigrant homes, where the nanny or housekeeper does not eat at the same table or even in the same room as the family.

What is curb appeal?

Curb appeals matters to Americans, and not just when it is time to sell your home. Curb appeal is how your home looks from the curb. You don't want to be the house with an overgrown lawn, junk on the front porch, paint chipping or other signs of neglect. If you don't have the time or skills to fix these yourself, hire someone. It may not seem important, but it is.

20

PARENTING IN AMERICA

How is the idea of a "good parent" different in
America than India?
In India, good parenting usually means providing a
good education for your child. Education is the top priority, for it is
the path to a good profession and, hopefully, a good life.

In America, the emotional and social well being of your child is
just as important as education. Parents see their role as developing
the "whole" child, not just the child's intellect. Indian children study
first and pursue interests if there is time remaining. "That's why
Indians aren't good at sports," one immigrant told me. The same
man said he feels less well rounded than his American co-workers
because they play instruments and sports that he does not.

You will hear American parents say they just want their child "to
be happy." This sounds nice, but there is a problem. Being happy as
a child is very different than being happy as an adult. Too much
focus on happiness in childhood can leave the child unprepared for
the hard work and discipline required to build a happy life as an
adult.

. . .

Beware of competitive Indian parents!

Quite a few of the Indian immigrants I interviewed said Indians back home are more helpful than Indian immigrants they meet in America. The women often feel this way, perhaps because women are more involved in the education of children. Other mothers are very competitive, they say. They will share information if you need a plumber, babysitter or pediatrician, but hold back information about tutors, summer camps, colleges or anything else that would give their child an advantage.

One interviewee admitted that she is competitive because in a country as populated as India, you have to be exceptional to move up in society. This mentality stayed with her, even after she came to America. She feels this is the reason why many Indian mothers are competitive. It makes sense. India is a competitive society, just like most of Asia. Test scores are made public, students are ranked, education is the way to advance in society. These are serious matters, and the results can affect a family for generations. Having a competitive edge is necessary for success in India, and it is not easy to lose that feeling when you come to America.

Still, this competitive attitude can make it hard to form real friendships. An Indian mom with high achieving children shared the view that in America there is more opportunity, so there is no need to be as competitive. She does not like that parents are secretive about certain types of information, and often avoids other Indian parents for this reason. Friendships that seem real could be fake, and parents of smart children are often used for information.

Some in the Indian community feel that competition is a sign that the family is new to America. Families who are financially secure and comfortably settled in America may adopt the American parenting style. Parents who have been in America for a while have learned that outward signs of competition are frowned upon by mainstream American society.

Competition is not limited to education, though. In India, who will succeed and who will fail seems more predictable, dictated by caste, access to power and family status. In America, nothing is predictable, and this creates insecurity. A wealthy family could fall into financial ruin in one generation. For Indian immigrants, especially those from privilege, this can be unsettling. As a result, they protect what is theirs and do not help newer immigrants. When immigrants from lower castes or less prestigious backgrounds succeed in America, sometimes others react with jealousy and resentment.

This is not to say the Indian community is not helpful - it can be a tremendous source of support, especially for those from similar regions of India.

Do kids in America have too much freedom?

Yes and no. Children here don't have the freedom to go outside and move freely through the neighborhood like they do in India. I've heard from interviewees that in parts of India you can say "go play outside" and you know your children will be safe. Families know each other's kids, and watch over them. That does not happen much in America anymore. Parents fear kidnappers, child molesters, bad influences like drugs and alcohol, crime and other dangers.

Kids are kept home with babysitters and watched more closely in America. Their time is scheduled, and afternoons are packed with activities. Strangers aren't trusted. Neighbors rarely "drop by" unannounced. If the parents work, older kids spend time alone at home.

American children have a lot of freedom when it comes to selecting their interests, studies, career and marriage partner. This worries some Indian parents. They see American students graduating from college and floundering without a set career path or marketable skills. They do not want their children to be lost in life, whereas some American parents will allow even adult children to take time to "find themselves."

For example, one Indian parent I spoke with was surprised that even top students go to college without first deciding on a career. She worries four years at college will be wasted if the students are not directed towards a career goal.

• • •

I don't want my kids to become too American. Is that OK?

Sure it's OK, but I'd try not to say this out loud. Many Americans would be offended.

Most of the immigrants I interviewed admit that living in America does accelerate the loss of cultural bonds. As one Indian immigrant told me, culture does not seem important when you are working and building a life in America. He warned, however, that there is a cost later in life. When his children became adults, he was saddened to realize they were not interested in his language, religion or cultural practices.

Part of American freedom is living the life you choose. It is completely possible to be an American and maintain your Indian culture. This is much easier today than it was for earlier immigrants, but it still takes time and effort.

Indian immigrants have told me that they wish Americans would understand why they want to continue cultural and religious activities after they come to America. This should not be seen as a threat or disrespect to American customs. According to one Indian immigrant, it is not that Americans don't accept the Indian culture, but more that they do not understand it.

I have heard Americans ask why immigrants come to America yet hold onto the customs from their home country. This reflects the American misunderstanding of why immigrants come. They do not come for baseball and hotdogs, they come for freedom and opportunity. Celebrating and learning from cultural differences is what makes America great - don't forget that no matter what you hear.

I am worried about negative influences on my child.

It can be difficult to figure out who is a good influence and who is not. The "good kids" don't always dress neatly or come from the "right" type of family. One Indian immigrant who came to the U.S. for college found this very confusing. At his boarding school in India, you could easily tell who the smart, good kids were. Not true in America. A good kid could come from a bad family, and might not dress or talk the way you expect. The doctor's kid in the advanced classes could be the one selling drugs and cheating.

Getting to know your kid's friends is very important. It is not just about who their parents are or their family status, but about who they are as people. I am always amused when I hear Indian parents describe their child's friend by first telling me the occupation of the friend's parents. "He must be a good kid because his father is a police officer." That's a big mistake.

The best way to learn about your kid's friends is to invite them over to your house. Observe how they act, how they treat your kid and others. Make your house a place where kids want to hang out. This means you have to be available, yes, but you can't outsource raising your kids in America. If you do, you may not like the result.

Spending time together as a family is another way to minimize negative influences. Children who eat dinner with their family on a regular basis not only learn manners and have better nutrition, but they also learn conversation skills. Studies show these children do better in school.

Limit screen time. American pediatricians recommend a limit of two hours per day. Keep the computer and television in a place where you can see what they are watching and doing online. Monitor social media and if they have a phone, set limits on what they can access without your permission.

Indian parents working to succeed in America may overlook the importance of being at home and spending time with heir kids. There is no substitute for being present - not just for the big events like birthdays, graduations and holidays, but for the quiet times, too. This is when your kids share what they are really feeling, and when you can have the greatest impact on them.

What about giving my children Indian names?

"Why did you give your kids such difficult names?"

An Indian immigrant I interviewed was asked this question by a non-Indian physician. Both of her children were born in America.

She explained that the names are Sanskrit words with special meaning for her. She also told him that Sanskrit is the world's oldest language.

"Still," he said, "you know Americans will have a hard time pronouncing those names."

Again, she explained the cultural and personal significance of the names.

Finally he said, "Will you let them change their names when they get older?"

"I hope they do not want to!" she told him.

This physician just did not get it. The names were not the problem. He was the problem. He did not like what was unfamiliar to him. If he would just respect her right to name her children and open his mind to the beauty of the names, no matter how unfamiliar, there would be no problem to speak of. We expect immigrants to adapt to an entirely different culture and we can't learn how to pronounce their names?

Is it true that young Americans don't respect their older family members?

Unfortunately, when both parents work outside the home, there is no choice but to hire strangers or use a nursing home to care for elderly parents. Support from neighbors and extended family is rare in America. Most people feel guilty about living far from their elderly parents or moving them to a nursing home.

Indians are aware of the stereotype of the disrespectful, selfish American child. After watching how an American family member cared for her ill father, an Indian doctor told me that he had never seen Indians care for their parents like that. He also expressed that these days you see more family fighting in India, partly because of the scarcity of resources. There is more competition and jealousy than before. The ties that bind the traditional "big Indian family" are becoming frayed, sadly.

One immigrant was surprised that American children use slang to speak with their parents. She found this disobedient, and thought children in India would not speak this way. However, on a recent trip back home she noticed that the way Indian children treat their parents is changing as well.

What is child protective services?

Before writing this book, I did not realize how many Indian immigrants fear that their children could be taken from them by the U.S. government. Could yelling, spanking or leaving the children alone outside to play be misunderstood as child abuse or neglect?

There is a government agency called "Child Protective Services" that is responsible for removing children from abusive homes. A confidential phone call or report from a school or hospital can start the process of investigation.

Of course, child abuse and neglect have different meanings in different cultures. The definition of child abuse under U.S. federal law is:

"Any recent act or failure to act on the part of a parent or care-taker, which results in death, serious physical or emotional harm, sexual abuse or exploitation, or an act or failure to act which presents an imminent risk of serious harm."

Indian parents can be strict, but I highly doubt any of their methods would be child abuse under this definition. While it is possible that strangers could misunderstand or overreact to your treatment of your child, child protective agencies are now more aware of cultural differences in parenting, especially in areas with a large immigrant population.

So I can give my kids a tupper?

For the most part, Americans disapprove of using physical force to discipline children.

If you chose to slap, hit or spank your child, don't do it in public, and don't talk about it. If the punishment leaves a mark, don't be surprised if your child's school calls with questions.

21

COMMUNICATION, BODY LANGUAGE & MANNERS

B efore writing this book, I assumed communication was one of the easier adjustments to life in America for Indian immigrants. After all, many Indians arrive already knowing basic English, and advanced English if they attended English medium schools. What I learned is that there is much more to communication than knowing English.

How is American English different than the English learned by Indians?

English is spoken in a particular way in America. Just as Indians tell me my Hindi is "book Hindi" and doesn't reflect spoken Hindi, the same is true for English. Americans use short forms of words, which can be confusing for immigrants. Some examples are "gimme" for "give me," "fam" for family, "rep" for representative, and "bro" for brother.

There are the sayings that just don't make sense - like "What's up?" and "Chill out" and "Give me a break."

The worst are the English expressions that have a negative

meaning in Hindi. One immigrant told me she was shocked to hear Americans use the greeting, "Hi." There is the closeness of the words "hug" and "hugna" - very different meanings. The most dangerous mixup is the swastika symbol from Hitler's Germany and the Hindu sign for peace. More on this later in the chapter.

How can I be careful not to offend others by making a language mistake?

The consequences for saying the wrong word is high in America, even if the mistake was innocent and did not mean to offend.

Indian immigrants tell me they fear offending others, and this makes them nervous to speak. So here are some rules to guide you:

First, never use a slang term to describe a group of people. Some examples of offensive slang terms that should never be spoken are: nigger (African-Americans), chink (Chinese), fag (homosexual), kike (Jew), wetback or spic (Hispanics), pussy, chick, bitch (woman). These are just examples - use the Internet to find the rest and stay away from them.

Next, speak to men and women in an equal manner. Never comment on a woman's appearance, or use words like "sweetheart," "honey," or other demeaning terms. If you are addressing men by their last names, do the same with women.

Don't make assumptions. A young woman with an older man may be his wife, not his daughter. A woman may be the boss, not an employee. A woman in a hospital could be the doctor, and the man could be the nurse (all female doctors share this complaint!). Someone dressed casually could be a CEO.

Most importantly, realize that nothing you say is private or protected. Men of a certain professional class may be able to speak freely in India, but that is not true in America. These days, everyone is held to the same standard. In an instant, successful business leaders and professionals who offend become a risk and liability for corporate boards, universities and other institutions. They are cut loose to save the reputation of the institution.

· · ·

So there is no such thing as an innocent mistake?

It's true that we learn from our mistakes, and nobody is perfect. Even if you follow my advice, there is going to be some word you don't know or some action that is perfectly acceptable in India but shunned here.

It happens to everyone, but it is a matter of degree. I've been embarrassed countless times because I didn't understand something about Indian culture, failed at chai, forgot to say "purnam" or confused the names "auntie," "chachi" and "mami" for the hundredth time. I feel like the stereotype of the "dumb American girl."

It's hard to learn a new culture. Nobody talks about it, but it is. That's why I wrote this book. There will be embarrassing moments, but hopefully they will be in the company of family, friends or kind strangers. Observe and learn what is offensive, since it changes often. If you aren't sure, ask someone you trust. If you do offend, apologize immediately, fix any misunderstanding and learn from it.

"I was joking" or "Don't be so sensitive" are never appropriate responses and will just make things worse. The same is true for stating that you are new to the country and don't understand the customs. To many Americans, this is not an excuse. They hold the view that, "You're in America now, follow our rules" or "You're not in India anymore." I don't like it, but I've heard this said many times.

Don't let a strong accent stop you from speaking.

It made me sad to hear an Indian immigrant mother tell me she never went to her daughter's school for the "guest reader" days. Parents are invited to class to read a book to the children. Because of her Indian accent, this mother was too shy to go, afraid that the children would not be able to understand her. There are other events she doesn't attend because she would be expected to speak, and not speaking would be considered rude. She wishes she could be more confident, but her accent holds her back.

This can also be about class differences within the Indian community, since Indians from villages without English medium schools may speak with a stronger accent. Language can reveal a lot about an Indian immigrant - education level, wealth, status, geographic region.

It's important not to let a strong accent silence you. This is not just important for your experience in America. It's also important that Americans hear your voice, your opinions, your story.

Are there dialects in America?

Different regions do produce different accents, but not dialects. Americans with different accents can still understand each other. For example, someone with a "Boston accent" might not fully pronounce the "r" sound, so car would sound like "cah." A Southerner may combine "you" and "all" to form the word "y'all."

I asked a recent Indian immigrant who did not attend an English medium school if English was hard for him. He laughed and said, "In India there are more than twenty languages and more than five hundred dialects. Here there is just English." Good point.

Is shaking hands the proper introduction?

American greeting customs are not very formal, but shaking hands has survived as the main way to show respect upon meeting a new person.

I was taught by my father to look a person in the eyes and give a "strong" handshake. He thought this made a good first impression. It was hard to know what this meant, though. I certainly didn't want to squeeze someone's hand too tightly, but it would be worse to have a weak or "limp" handshake.

Looking back, I think the "strong handshake" is more of a male than female thing. To be honest, I don't pay much attention to the strength of a handshake anymore. In fact, if a handshake is so strong that I notice it, I might be a little afraid of that person. Do what feels right. Extend your hand, but don't worry about the grip.

. . .

What if I can't shake hands?

Some Muslims and other religions forbid contact between male and female strangers. This makes shaking hands difficult. The Muslim population in America is not large, so Americans are unfamiliar with this restriction. However, a simple explanation and a smile should fix any misunderstanding. Use whatever greeting makes you comfortable, and add that you do not mean any disrespect by not shaking hands.

Even non-Muslims find themselves in this situation. One immigrant school teacher had to think quick when a male opened his arms for a hug. It was the end of the school year, and the teachers were saying good bye for the summer. She took a small step back and explained that hugging him was not allowed in her culture.

"That's cool," he said. He respected her custom and did not try to hug her again. They are still good friends.

What are other acceptable greetings?

Saying "hi" or "hello" with a wave of the hand is probably the most common greeting.

Americans are big huggers. Older Americans sometimes kiss each other on the cheek. Friends high-five each other. President Obama made the "fist bump" popular.

Don't cut the line, please!

One immigrant laughed as he told me that back in India, pushing ahead and cutting the line is a good thing, even an act to be proud of.

Cutting the line is rude and disrespectful in America. Sure, it still happens, but it will be followed by others yelling, "Hey, you cut the line!" Wait your turn.

. . .

How do I show respect for an elder?

Unfortunately, you may see Americans treat elders in ways that would never happen in India. There is no touching feet to show respect, no adding *ji* to the end of a name or even standing when an elder person enters the room.

That said, the traditional ways of showing respect to any person, not just an elder, are introducing yourself (handshake if possible), using the person's correct name and title, not interrupting and using polite phrases like "Excuse me," "Please," and "Thank you." It is polite to offer an older person or a pregnant woman your seat if none are available, and to hold the door for them. If you do not know the person, use the titles Mr. or Mrs./Ms. instead of calling them by their first name alone.

What about speaking the language from my home country in public?

I strongly advise you to speak English at all times in the workplace, even during breaks. I've seen Americans roll their eyes at co-workers speaking Spanish in the cafeteria. Some of this is because they don't know what is being said in Spanish, and fear they could be the subject of the conversation.

While I understand that speaking your native language is comfortable and natural, especially in a new country, many Americans are annoyed by this. Just be aware that if you are in a mixed group of English and non-English speakers, the English speaker may find your use of another language rude. In their eyes, by not speaking English you are saying you don't want to talk to them.

You can't miss the use of English and Spanish for signs, forms and announcements in America. This began in the 1990's, and not all Americans like it. In the view of these Americans, earlier immigrant groups had to learn English and the same should be true for today's Spanish immigrants.

· · ·

What about body language rules between men and women?

Before I got off the plane in Patna, my mother-in-law told me not to hold my new husband's hand in public. She had never said this to me in the U.S., and didn't mention it when we landed in New Delhi. That was 2003, and my mother-in-law is probably more traditional than the average Indian. She may have even been fearing for my safety, since I was the only white person we saw in Patna during our trip. I'm sure if we went to Patna today we would see couples holding hands.

In America, it is acceptable for married and dating couples (including same sex couples) to hold hands, slow dance, cuddle and kiss in public. It is not surprising to see a man touch his girlfriend or wife's hair or shoulder with affection, or caress her belly if she is pregnant.

You may hear the term "chivalry" or it's more popular use in the phrase "Chivalry is dead." Chivalry was the code of conduct for the knights of King Arthur. It generally refers to a gentleman, one who opens the door for women, helps them with packages, pulls out their chair, pays for dinner.

Now, keep in mind that you hear "Chivalry is dead" because most men don't act like knights from King Arthur's table, and many women don't want them to. Some women find this condescending because it treats women like they are "weaker" than men. However, you won't be called a sexist or offend women if you make these polite gestures.

Gender separation is viewed with great suspicion in America. Even though men and women naturally separate at many Indian social events, keep in mind that to some Americans this will appear to be a forced separation that signals a lesser treatment and respect for women.

What do Americans mean by "personal space"?

If someone asks you to give them space, they mean you are too physically close to them. This can be hard for Indians coming from a very crowded country. America is the only place in the world where space is such a big deal, one Indian immigrant told me. Another said, "Americans have all these issues with space."

It's true. You feel like a criminal if you bump into someone and don't say excuse me right away. Even if there is just the possibility of contact, Americans will say excuse me. We tell our children to "keep their hands to themselves" and teach them to walk on the correct side of the street. The wrong kind of touching - a touch on the leg, brush against the chest or hand on the cheek or shoulder - can be offensive or even sexual misconduct.

How much space is enough? This is one for the "follow the crowd" rule. It's better to give more space than less. A person can always ask you to come closer.

A word on body odor

This isn't much of a challenge for today's Indian immigrant, but it was in the past and the stereotype has stuck.

To Americans, body odor is a sign of uncleanliness. It can be a one-way ticket to social isolation. The body odor of an Indian valet was even the subject the popular American television show *Seinfeld*. When Seinfeld picked up his car from the valet, the smell was so bad that he could not even give the car away.

My husband never fell victim to the body odor plague, but knows it well. He has a hypothesis, as I'm sure ever Indian does. He thinks the smell is partly caused by cumin, and partly by Indian cooking odors that seep into clothing. There are certainly enough deodorant products in America to tame even the fiercest odor.

Don't worry - Indians aren't the only ones with body odor. Some Americans smell worse than any cumin consuming Indian.

When is it OK to eat with my hands?

If utensils are given to you with the food, then use them. There is a category of food called "finger foods" - French fries, mozzarella sticks, chips, small appetizers, hot dogs, hamburgers, pizza. When Americans eat with their hands, they use both left and right, and place their napkin on their lap before eating.

We use too many plastic utensils in America. Eating with the hands really is better for the environment and sometimes more efficient. Still, this is not accepted in America.

Americans feel so strongly about table manners that they will scold children by saying, "Don't eat with your hands - you're not an animal!"

Is it rude not to tip?

Not tipping at all is considered extremely rude. Americans generally tip a minimum of 15% of the bill for service professionals like waiters, cab drivers, delivery people, barbers and hair salons.

Even if the service is not satisfactory, a small tip is better than no tip. People working in these professions are often paid less because the employer assumes the public will make up the difference with tips.

Is it rude to correct the pronunciation of my name?

No, not at all. You will probably have to do this a lot. Here's how it usually goes:

The American will say, "Sorry if I am mispronouncing/butchering your name" before attempting to say it. Upon hearing this, you are expected to laugh politely and say, "It's ok." Then you can offer the correct pronunciation, and they will likely repeat it a few times, nod their head, and then mispronounce it!

Everyone thinks I am nodding no when I am nodding yes!

Those of us with Indian family and friends know the famous Indian "side nod" or "head bobble," but most Americans do not. They see the side nod and think you are shaking your head no in disagreement.

.   .   .

Be very careful with the Hindu swastika symbol.

Ever since Adolf Hitler stole the swastika symbol and used it for the Nazi party, it has represented hatred, anti-semitism and inhumanity in the world. It creates fear and terror in the hearts of Americans. If you use this symbol outside of a religious ceremony or with people who do not appreciate its Hindu significance, you will suffer shame and possible harm as a result. I advise against using it on the entrance of your home or in public. It is just too dangerous.

Anything else on manners?

Despite what you may see in American movies, burping and farting in public is not appropriate. Cover your mouth when you yawn, sneeze, cough and burp (if you absolutely have to burp in public).

Don't ever call anyone fat or old, even if they are. When I was young I innocently asked a neighbor if she was pregnant. Horrified, my mother made me apologize and I was punished. This was just for the suggestion that the woman was fatter than usual around the belly. In some cultures fat is a sign of wealth and health. American is not one of them.

Comments on skin color are also inappropriate. "Fair skin" may be a compliment in India, but not in America. It is tinged with racism, and misses the mark on American beauty standards. Americans don't want to be pale. They think rosy cheeks and a tan complexion are healthy and beautiful.

A co-worker of mine recently made a comment about bathroom manners that left me speechless. She said that her former employer hired a lot of "immigrant workers" and they "did not follow proper bathroom manners." I had no idea what she meant. When I asked, she whispered that people from other countries don't always flush the toilet. It was ridiculous. I have worked with people from all over the world and never experienced this. I highly doubt that immigrants were the reason for the dirty bathrooms, but it does show you that Americans often carry the assumption that immigrants don't share our standards of cleanliness.

Use polite terms like please, thank you and excuse me. It is important for children to use these as well, and to learn to share at a young age.

22

STEREOTYPES (LAZY THINKING)

"Jewish people are cheap."
"Blacks are lazy."
"Latinos come to the country illegally."
"Blondes are dumb."
"Indians have body odor and are good in math and science."

Statements like these are what I call lazy thinking. That's what I consider stereotypes - we get lazy and see people as groups with the same characteristics, rather than seeing each individual for what he or she is. All people get lazy like this, not just Americans. However, I thought it would be helpful for you to know about the stereotypes for two reasons. First, so that you do not fall into the lazy thinking yourself, and second, to know what stereotypes non-Indians may hold about you.

Beware of people that use stereotypes to divide Americans.

People use stereotypes to serve their own agendas, whether it is the media trying to attract attention or politicians turning people against each other. You will see it everywhere - wealthy vs. working class, white vs. black, citizen vs. immigrant.

Don't be easy to fool. The ones putting out these messages are not thinking about the long-term damage to the country. After the election is over or the news program has cashed in on high ratings, we are left with a divided, weak public with outdated, simplistic and lazy opinions.

But aren't stereotypes based on some truth?

Yes, stereotypes are true for some people in a group, but NOT all. That is the point.

Most stereotypes were formed years ago and just never died. For example, over the past fifteen years Indians have improved tremendously in the area of body odor. Still, last week I heard people joking that Indians smell bad. Maybe a few still do, but come on. Just because stereotypes stick around does not make them true for everyone.

How should I react if I hear stereotypes?

"Not all _____ are like that."

What do Americans know about Indians?

Lazy thinking led a woman to ask an Indian immigrant professional, "Where are your bangles?" This lady did not wear bangles to work, but the person asking her assumed Indians wear bangles all the time. This Indian said that often Americans do not understand that there are many different types of Indians. Another American told her there is no difference between Pakistanis, Bangladeshis or Indians because "they all look the same." Again, lazy thinking. She patiently explained the differences.

The truth is Americans do not learn much about India in school or on the news. We learn about Gandhi, but nothing about modern

India. Unless they seek out information about India on their own, Americans are left with stereotypes in the media or generalizations about what they see in front of them (the Indian gas station or mini-mart owner, the Indian cab driver, the Indian doctor).

When India appears in popular culture, Americans rarely see the successful parts of India. For example, when the show "Amazing Race" stops in India during the trip around the world, none of the images are positive about the country (other than the friendly people!). Movies like Slumdog Millionaire also show Americans a single stereotype of life in India. For an Indian news story to reach American viewers, chances are high that it involves an honor killing or rape. I know there has been incredible growth and success in India over the past decade, but the average American is not getting the full story.

So what are the stereotypes about Indians immigrants?

There are positive and negative stereotypes about Indian immigrants. I'll start with the positive. Many Americans view Indians as hard working and friendly. Indians are diligent students who excel in math and science. The negative stereotypes are that Indians are dirty, smelly (food and body odor) and since 9/11 some people hold the stereotype that Indians are terrorists. A more recent stereotype is that Indians are taking tech jobs from Americans.

There you have it. The ugly things lazy thinkers may believe about Indians. Hopefully you will never be faced with this, but at least now you are prepared.

Indian Americans tell me it is necessary to have a "thick skin" and not let ignorant comments based on stereotypes affect you. They are often surprised that Americans are easily offended and ignorant words can end friendships and careers.

Indians who have been told to "Go back to your country" or called terrorists tend to laugh it off and do not make a big deal about it. Perhaps this is because they are confident that they are on the path to success, and will not be stopped or even distracted by others. One Indian doctor told me about an experience with a cashier at Walmart. The cashier may have been trying to make her feel unwelcome and uncomfortable, but in the big picture, the Indian was living a much better life financially than the Walmart cashier, and that might be why she found it more amusing than insulting.

Another Indian doctor shared that after 9/11 a patient said all of "them" (immigrants) should be kicked out of the country. "I am one of them," she responded. "You don't count, doc," the patient said. This is an example of how personal relationships can be the antidote to stereotypes.

What stereotypes do Americans have about their fellow Americans?

Most of these are at the top of the chapter, but I'll expand on them.

Jewish stereotypes involve money. Jews are seen as good with money, but this positive stereotype quickly turns negative, calling Jews greedy and cheap. Conspiracy theorists claim Jews control finance and the media and manipulate them to further Jewish interests (anti-Arab, pro-Israel). There are even Holocaust deniers who claim the Holocaust never happened, despite overwhelming historic evidence and person narratives to the contrary.

American stereotypes about blacks involve laziness, which is beyond ridiculous when you recall that slaves worked harder than any Americans and the success of this country came from their hard work. Yet, the stereotype exists that blacks are lazy and live on free government handouts. Some of the most insidious stereotypes even go so far as to say that blacks are genetically inferior to whites.

President Trump used Latino stereotypes during the 2016 election, and still does. Describing those crossing the border as rapists, gang members and criminals helped him turn many Americans against these immigrants.

Muslims suffer from the stereotype that they are extremists and can't be trusted.

While you might think the stereotype of Chinese and Koreans as hard-working and studious is a positive, it must not be if schools like Harvard are saying that admitting too many Asians is a negative.

I don't know any Indian who wants to be a lazy thinker, so don't believe stereotypes.

23

RELIGION IN AMERICA

T he Pilgrims came for religious freedom and this freedom is
protected in our Constitution. Still, you will hear the claim
that America is a "Christian nation." Yes, the majority religion in America is Christianity, but the founding fathers who wrote
the Constitution feared the "tyranny of the majority" not only in
politics, but religion as well.

What is the separation of church and state?

The Bill of Rights (first ten amendments to the Constitution)
protects both the *free exercise of religion* and *freedom from religion*. This
means that the government cannot interfere with you practicing
your religion or with your choice not to practice any religion.

Every freedom in the Constitution is weighed against public
safety. So, if your Diwali celebration causes fires that threaten public
safety, the government can stop you from overdoing it with the
diyas. Fireworks are illegal in some states, so you would not be able
to light fireworks for Diwali, even though it is a religious celebration.
But if you are celebrating Diwali responsibly, the government
cannot stop you.

There can be no "state religion" in America, and the government cannot push a religious agenda or punish citizens who do not participate in religion. Remember, the Pilgrims came because they were being persecuted by the King of England for objecting to the Church of England. Religious freedom was central to the very formation of the country.

Is America a religious country?

According to a 2014 report on "Religion and Public Life" by the Pew Research Center, the percentage of Americans who identify as belonging to a religious group is on the decline. The exceptions are Hinduism and Islam, and this is explained by the number of immigrants coming to America holding these faiths. From 2007 to 2014, the percentage of Americans identifying as Christian has dropped from about 78% to 70%. The chart below shows the representation of religions in America in 2014, as reported by the Pew study.

Christian - 70.6%

Jewish - 1.9%

Muslim - .9%

Buddhist - .7%

Hindu - .7%

No religion - 15.6%

Why do Americans confuse Hindus and Muslims?

This will be a surprise for you coming from India, where the line separating Muslims and Hindus is clear and runs deep. In the U.S., if you have brown skin and are not black or Hispanic, many Americans will assume you are Muslim, and if you are Muslim, they will fear you are an extremist. Americans see a Sikh's turban and think Arab even though Arabs don't wear turbans. There are people in my family who think my husband is Muslim, even though we had a Hindu wedding and have been married for fifteen years.

.   .   .

Do Muslims and Hindus mix in America?

In many ways, this depends on how long your family has lived in America. Indians who were raised in India often carry a mistrust of Hinduism or Islam with them to America, especially if they lived through the pain of the Partition. The next generation may interact more with those from the other faith at school and work. These friendships replace the stereotypes and prejudices of newer immigrants. Furthermore, the shared experience of being non-white in America can form strong bonds despite religious differences.

Who are black Muslims?

It is estimated that 15-30% of slaves brought to America from Africa by the slave trade were of the Muslim faith. Throughout the South, Christianity was often imposed on slaves by slave owners to keep slaves obedient and docile. Even with forced conversions to Christianity, Islam survived in the black community. The most famous black Muslim group in America is the Nation of Islam. Malcolm X belonged to the Nation of Islam before he was assassinated in 1965. The Nation of Islam has been praised for work in urban centers, but is also criticized for the anti-Semitic and divisive views of its leader, Louis Farrakhan.

What is the difference between Catholics and Protestants?

There were no Protestants before the German monk Martin Luther's "protest" against the Catholic Church in the early 1500's. Luther's objections to the Catholic Church marked the beginning of the Protestant Reformation in Europe. The Pilgrims were Protestant, and sailed to America to escape the religious turmoil between Protestants and Catholics.

Catholicism in America is in many ways the religion of immigrants. The number of Catholics began to rise when Irish and Italian immigrants settled in America. Catholics faced discrimination and skepticism. The religion did not become mainstream in America until after the election of John F. Kennedy. The Kennedy family is now considered American royalty, but in the early years their Catholic faith and Irish immigrant roots kept them out of upper class society. Today, Hispanics are the majority of younger Catholics, and their numbers are increasing. Catholics are 20% of the U.S. population, compared to 26% evangelical Christian and 46% other Protestant faiths.

Some of the major differences between Catholics and Protestants are that the pope is the leader of the Catholic Church, women cannot serve as priests and priests cannot marry. Nuns are the female leaders in the Catholic Church, but their duties are not equal to priests and they also cannot marry. Communion is the center of the Catholic mass. Catholic leaders also take a strong position on social issues such as abortion and homosexuality. In Protestant churches, women serve in leadership positions, and church leaders can marry. Protestants do not follow the pope.

What is a WASP?

This means "White Anglo Saxon Protestant," the dominant ethnic and religious group throughout much of U.S. history.

Who are Mormons?

The Church of Jesus Christ of Latter-Day Saints, known as the Mormon Church, is said to be the only purely American religion. The religion is based on Joseph Smith's claim that he received gold plates with Christian texts not included in the Bible that he translated into the Book of Mormon and published in 1830. The plates were found in the U.S., and describe Jesus' appearance in the U.S. Smith also claimed the Garden of Eden was in the U.S.

The religion has been criticized for allowing polygamy, but this was outlawed by the church in 1890. Mormons follow a health code and do not smoke, drink alcohol, coffee or tea or use illegal drugs. Mormons are the fourth largest Christian group in the U.S. They are active missionaries outside the U.S., and more than half of their members do not live in the U.S.

Perhaps the most famous Mormon is Mitt Romney, former governor of Massachusetts who ran against Barack Obama in 2012 (challenging Obama's second term). Romney is currently a senator from Utah. People became a bit more comfortable and familiar with Mormons after this election.

What is evangelical Christianity (also called "born again" or "non-denominational")?

At 25% of the population, evangelical Christians are the largest religious group in the U.S. This Christian group is also called "born again" or "non-denominational." The term "born again" means these Christians have a spiritual "rebirth" upon accepting Jesus Christ as their savior. "Non-denominational" means that evangelicals do not belong to a "denomination" of Christianity such as Catholic, Baptist, Lutheran, Methodist or others. The term "evangelical" comes from "evangelize," which means to convert to Christianity. They are politically active, with more than 50% affiliating with the Republican Party.

What is the Black Church?

There is no "black church." This term refers to predominantly black churches that served as the core of black social and political activity dating back to the days of slavery.

Slaves were not allowed to gather together in the same place, but in some areas they were allowed to meet for Christian worship in segregated black churches. The church became the center of the black community, not just for worship but for socializing and political organizing. It was common for blacks to pool their money to build and support the church. Men and women excluded from leadership in white society became leaders in the black church. These churches made the Civil Rights Movement possible - and successful. It is for this reason that they were burned and bombed by opponents of the Movement.

The predominantly black churches could be any Christian

denomination such as Methodist, Baptist or African Methodist Episcopal (AME). These churches do not exclude whites or other races.

What are different types of Judaism?

The three main sects of Judaism are orthodox, conservative and reformed. The largest number of Jews are reformed. The main difference is how strictly the group follows the Jewish holy book, the Torah. In orthodox services, men and women sit separately and women do not serve as rabbis.

Hasidic Jews are a very strict sect of Judaism from Eastern Europe. There is a large Hasidic population in Brooklyn, New York. Hasidic men and women are separated in school, temple and other aspects of life.

What is anti-Semitism?

A Jewish relative of mine who lives in Europe shared with me that in her view, the only safe places for Jews today are the U.S. and Israel. Prejudice, hatred and violence towards Jews is known as anti-Semitism, and is still common in the U.S. and around the world.

In the U.S., you will see a range of anti-Semitic activity. You may hear comments like, "Don't be such a Jew," or much worse. "Fire up the gas chamber," was said to a Jewish student in my Long Island town, invoking the horror of the Holocaust. People use the word "Jew" as a synonym for cheap. You will also see anti-Semitic graffiti such as swastikas on temples and public buildings. Vandalism against Jewish temples is often seen on the news. Then, there are the Holocaust deniers and the white supremacists. The leading chant at the 2017 "Unite the Right" rally in Charlottesville, Virginia was "Jews will not replace us." In the fall of 2018 a gunman shouting "All Jews must die" killed eleven Jews in a synagogue in Pittsburgh, Pennsylvania.

Many are confused by President Trump's response to anti-Semitic crimes. He is slow to criticize and denounce them, if he does so at all. Some say this is because neo-Nazis, white supremacists and other anti-Semites support him politically. Still, President Trump's daughter converted to Judaism, and his grandchildren are Jewish. His tolerance of anti-Semitism is making the world more dangerous for his family.

Hare Krishnas in the US

Swami Prabhupada brought Hare Krishna to the U.S. in 1966 and called the American branch the International Society of Krishna Consciousness ("ISKCON"). This group attracted the counter-culture 1960's "hippie" generation, including the famous musician George Harrison. However, its public image was harmed after a child molestation lawsuit in the 1970's. Today, Hare Krishnas are a fringe group in America and not as visible as before. Many Americans view Hare Krishnas as a cult, and unfortunately do not understand the differences between Hare Krishnas and mainstream Hindus.

What is secular Buddhism?

The generation of the 1960's was curious about eastern religions. Young people traveled to India to learn about meditation and Buddhism. These people returned to the U.S. and began the mindfulness movement, which is very popular today. Some were practicing Buddhists, but others used the tools of Buddhism to break patterns of thinking, manage stress and create compassion. This is known as secular (non-religious) Buddhism. Some of the well known leaders of this movement were John Kabbat Zinn, Joseph Goldstein and Sharon Salzberg.

The Dali Lama is popular in the U.S. His books are best sellers, and when he speaks he sells out stadiums. These Americans are not monks or practicing Buddhists, but embrace the Dali Lama's message of peace and forgiveness.

What is the difference between atheist and agnostic?

An atheist does not believe in God. An agnostic isn't sure whether God exists or not.

Has there ever been an atheist or agnostic president?

Maybe, but they didn't show it. These days, especially to win broad support, politicians speak about their religion.

24

CULTURAL TRADITIONS, HOLIDAYS & CELEBRATIONS

"Can I wish a woman other than my wife a happy Valentine's Day?"

"What is a baby shower?"

"Are Easter and Passover the same thing?"

These are just some of the questions Indian immigrants ask about American holidays and celebrations. We don't have as many festivals as India, that is for sure. The major American holidays and celebrations are explained below.

What is a federal holiday?

On "federal" holidays, the government is closed. This includes government services such as mail and garbage collection. Schools and libraries are closed. Private business owners are not required to give workers the day off on federal holidays.

National Holidays

. . .

Thanksgiving (third Thursday in November)

The good thing about Thanksgiving is that everyone celebrates this holiday. That is what makes it a true American holiday. It is not a religious holiday, and giving thanks is a universal concept. It's a federal holiday, and the Wednesday before Thanksgiving is often the busiest travel day of the year.

However, don't expect to enjoy the food on Thanksgiving. In many ways the food is the focus of the day, but the traditional turkey dinner is a bland and tasteless meal. At least that's how the Indians I know describe it. I didn't realize it myself until my husband's first Thanksgiving with my family, which I talk about in the *Food* chapter.

Of course, this turkey obsession ignores the fact that many Indians are vegetarian. Even those who eat turkey are restricted by the Hindu "no bird on Thursday" rule, which I did not know about until recently.

What is the Thanksgiving story?

The Pilgrims who sailed to America on the Mayflower did not know how to live off the land. They were urban, not farming people. Half died after their first winter in America (Massachusetts). There were only fifty-two Pilgrims left by the time of the first Thanksgiving.

Without the Native Americans, in particular Squanto (Tisquantum) and Samoset, the Pilgrims would not have survived. Squanto and Samoset spoke English and showed the Pilgrims how to farm, hunt and fish. The first harvest meal shared by the Pilgrims and Native Americans is what is known as the Thanksgiving meal. In my view, the thanks owed on Thanksgiving is to the Native Americans who saved the Pilgrims from extinction.

Martin Luther King, Jr. Day (third Monday of January)

The popular understanding of Martin Luther King, Jr. Day is this - Martin Luther King, Jr. led the non-violent Civil Rights Movement and was assassinated in 1968 at age 39. He used peaceful means to fight discrimination and segregation in the South. He made the world a better place. End of story.

Much is left out of this story. The fight for civil rights in the United States was violent, bloody and ugly. Even establishing the federal holiday to honor the birthday of Martin Luther King, Jr. (January 15), took fifteen years, and even after Ronald Reagan made it official, states resisted.

Martin Luther King, Jr. was not a universally beloved figure when he was alive. The government spied on him and smeared his reputation. They called him un-American, an extremist and a communist national security threat. The famous March on Washington where King gave his "I Have a Dream" speech only had favorable support from 23% of Americans.[1] A majority of Americans thought the tactics of the Civil Rights Movement were hurting blacks and had gone too far. After the passage of the Voting rights Act, only 36% of whites considered Martin Luther King, Jr. a help to the cause of civil rights. As King moved his focus to economic inequality, military spending in Vietnam and civil rights in the North, his popularity plummeted even more. White counter-protestors with vicious signs were common at his appearances. This was not a minority - the majority of Americans were opposed to King.

Another reality that is omitted from the myth of Martin Luther King, Jr. is that it took a long time for the changes promised in the Voting Rights Act of 1965 and Civil Rights Act of 1964 to become a reality. You may have seen pictures of black children desegregating white schools. Want to know what happened after? Whites left. Ruby Bridges, who integrated a public school in Louisiana, was taught alone, in a classroom of one. We don't hear about that.

President's Day (third Monday of February)

This federal holiday was originally created to celebrate the birthday of the first president, George Washington (February 22), but later included Abraham Lincoln's birthday (February 21) and now is a day to celebrate all American presidents.

· · ·

Memorial Day (last Monday in May)

On this federal holiday Americans remember those who died in battle fighting for the United States. The Civil War was the greatest loss of life for Americans, at nearly 500,000. The next highest is World War II with about 300,000. Memorial day is also known as the unofficial start of the summer season.

Veteran's Day (November 11)

Veterans Day honors all Americans who served in the Armed Forces - known as veterans. This federal holiday is broader than Memorial Day because it honors veterans alive and dead.

Labor Day (first Monday in September)

Labor Day began over one hundred years ago as a way for American trade and labor organizers to bring together workers for a day of rest and celebration. In the late 1800's, communist and Marxist ideas had reached America. Laborers were organizing into unions, and fought for an eight hour workday and six day work week, among other protections. Labor Day was a way to recognize and appreciate the contributions of workers to society. It is a federal holiday and also known as the end of the summer season.

Fourth of July

This holiday is also known as Independence Day because the Declaration of Independence was signed on July 4, 1776. Although celebrated for years with parades, fireworks and concerts, the Fourth of July did not become a federal holiday until 1941.

An interesting historic fact is that founding fathers Thomas Jefferson and John Adams both died on July 4th, exactly fifty years after they signed the Declaration of Independence.

· · ·

Christian Holidays
Christmas (December 25)

Christmas is the biggest holiday in the U.S. It's not just because a majority of Americans are Christian. Most Americans celebrate Christmas, regardless of their religion. Christmas has become a secular holiday, celebrated with light decorations, carols, Christmas trees and of course, gifts. Many Indian immigrants celebrate Christmas. Some Christians prefer to keep Christmas a religious holiday, which explains the clever bumper sticker "Keep Christ in Christmas."

Every year the Christmas season starts earlier, allowing businesses to cash in on the holiday. Many businesses make their money for the entire year during the Christmas season. What I don't like about Christmas is the cruel hoax we play on children by insisting on the existence of Santa Claus - the white bearded, jolly man in a red suit who delivers gifts to children on Christmas Eve. "Spoiling" the myth of Santa Claus is a high crime for American kids. Even though the Santa myth is illogical, don't let your kids be the ones who tell the truth to other kids. They should play along to survive.

Easter (Spring holiday, but date varies)

Unlike with Christmas, Easter is only celebrated by Christians. The holiday marks the resurrection of Jesus to heaven after he was killed on Earth. The resurrection is the most important tenet of the Christian faith - believers cite it as proof that Jesus was the son of God.

Ash Wednesday marks the start of Lent, the forty days leading up to Easter Sunday. You will see Christians with a cross of ashes on their foreheads on Ash Wednesday. The ashes are distributed at church services and represent that we will all return to ash one day. During Lent, Christians deprive themselves of a treat (like chocolate) as preparation for Easter.

Just like Christmas, Easter has a fictional character that delivers gifts for children. The Easter Bunny delivers treats to children on

Easter morning. Unlike Christmas, Easter is not a secular holiday. Non-Christians do not give their children Easter treats or go on Easter egg hunts.

Easter is not a good holiday for Jews. Throughout history violence against Jews increases during the Easter season. This is because some Christians blame Jews for the crucifixion of Jesus thousands of years ago.

Other Christian Celebrations

You will probably hear talk about Christian children receiving "baptism," "first communion" and "confirmation." These rituals are significant events in the life of a young Christian.

Jewish Holidays
Hanukkah or Chanukah (determined by Hebrew calendar, usually in December)

This eight night celebration is known as the Festival of Lights. Centuries ago, while the Jewish people were at war in Jerusalem, they only had enough oil for their menorah to last one night. To their amazement, the menorah remained lit for eight nights. This is known as the "Hanukkah Miracle." To celebrate, Jews light a menorah for eight nights and mark each night with a special gift.

Passover (early Spring)

Passover is a Jewish holiday celebrating the liberation of Jews from Egyptian slavery. The stories of Moses leading the Jews to freedom found in the Old Testament of the Bible are as as central to the Jewish religion as the Mahabharata is to Hinduism.

Passover is celebrated with a "seder" - a meal to which non-Jews are often invited. It is a kind gesture to be invited to a seder, and the respectful response is to attend.

. . .

Other Jewish Celebrations

You may be invited to a bat-mitzvah (for Jewish girls) or bar-mitzvah (for Jewish boys). These involve a ceremony at the temple and party afterwards. The bat or bar mitzvah marks when females (age 12) or males (age 13) become adults in the eyes of the Jewish religion.

Yom Kippur occurs in early October and is known as the "Day of Atonement." On this solemn day, Jews repent for their sins. Rosh Hashanah, also in the early fall, is the Jewish New Year celebration. In areas with a significant Jewish population, schools are closed on these holy days.

Non-Religious Holidays

Valentine's Day (February 14)

School children and couples celebrate this holiday with cards and sweets. It is an innocent holiday for children - all of the children exchange cards, and there is no talk of betrothing or arranging! Couples celebrate with cards and gifts. Some people wear red or pink on Valentine's Day, and the angel Cupid is the symbol of the day.

To answer the question at the top of the chapter, it is only appropriate to wish a Happy Valentine's Day to your romantic partner and perhaps your children.

St. Patrick's Day (March 17)

This holiday isn't just for the Irish anymore, but that is how it started. Irish immigrants did not have an easy time in America. They were poor and arrived from the early 1800's to the early 1900's. For most of the nineteenth century the Irish were the main immigrant group in America, and they were targeted by the Ku Klux Klan (KKK) and other anti-immigrant groups.

St. Patrick's Day was a way for Irish immigrants to be proud of their culture and celebrate in a land that acted like it didn't want them. These days, you don't have to be Irish to celebrate. There are parades and lots of beer drinking. Green is everywhere - the rivers of Chicago are dyed green, as are food and drink items. People also wear green to celebrate the holiday.

Mardi Gras (day before Ash Wednesday)

Mardi Gras is celebrated in New Orleans, Louisiana. It is by far the biggest American carnival. Also known as "Fat Tuesday," Mardi Gras is a joyous, rollicking celebration that has several meanings. It is the last party before Lent begins, but also celebrates spring and fertility. The Mardi Gras parades are legendary and bring up to a million tourists to New Orleans.

Halloween (October 31)

Halloween is a strange holiday, but the kids love it. This is because they can dress up in costumes, knock on anybody's door and fully expect to receive free candy as a result. I can understand why someone not knowing this custom might slam the door, close the blinds or tell kids to go away. This happened to us once, actually, in a neighborhood for international graduate students. A mob of children dressed as ghosts and princesses demanding candy can be alarming.

Halloween is the day before All Saints Day, a Christian holiday honoring saints. Saints are voted into sainthood by the leadership of the Catholic church because of their faith and good works.

Trick-or-treating is generally safe, depending on the neighborhood. Make sure you have candy ready. You can leave it at the front door if you are taking your kids out. I have noticed that fewer children trick or treat every year. This could be because communities host Halloween events where kids can get candy without going door to door. For my kids, the thrill is ringing a stranger's doorbell to get candy. It is also a good way to meet your neighbors!

25

CLOTHING

What should I know about clothes in the workplace?
Clothing is one of the ways people make a first impression about you. A doctor friend who is always beautifully dressed told me she must dress well to be taken seriously. My mother-in-law feels uncomfortable in "western" clothes. Still, she wears them when she leaves home for business.

Workplace attire in America is more casual than it used to be, but is still conservative. In the courtroom and most boardrooms, a dark suit is the norm. You may hear the term "business casual" - this means less formal than a suit, but not as casual as jeans or weekend clothes. In younger companies, dress is usually more relaxed. However, I wouldn't start dressing casual from the beginning. I would take the lead from others in your position. Mark Zuckerberg and other tech company founders may wear hooded sweatshirts and jeans, but that doesn't mean you can.

It is rare to see Indian clothing or other ethnic clothing in the workplace. I have worked in major cities with diverse populations, and I have never seen a salwar kameez in the office or during my commute. These clothes are kept for the weekends and social events.

What I have seen in the office environment is 24 karat Indian jewelry (including bangles), nose earrings, *sindoor* on the scalp and *mehndi* on the hands. After my wedding and other family weddings, I go to work with *mehndi* on my hands. My co-workers are always delighted and interested. The appearance of my hands is not an integral part of my job, though. If I was a hand model, my employer would have the right to object because the *mehndi* prevents me from doing my job.

Am I allowed to wear traditional dress at work if I want to?

You are only restricted from wearing a garment in the workplace if it presents a safety hazard or interferes with your work. So, if you work in a factory and your sari keeps getting caught in the equipment, your boss can legally require you to wear something else to prevent this from happening. Also, if a job requires a uniform or specific type of clothing, you must conform with those rules if you want the job.

This reasoning applies to individuals wearing burqas and hijabs as well. The *hijab*/headscarf question is not as hotly debated in the U.S. as it is in Europe, perhaps because our Muslim population is much lower.

Can I wear sandals (chappals) to work?

My mother-in-law was used to wearing sandals (*chappals*) all year in India. She would wear *chappals* everywhere, even to work as a professor. In America, sandals - open toed shoes - are not as acceptable. First, it is too cold to wear sandals many months of the year. Second, most offices do not allow sandals, even in the summer months.

My mother-in-law bought western shoes and hated them. She got blisters. Her feet hurt all the time. She never got used to them. Now, she works from home and wears her *chappals*. In the winter, she simply wears heavy socks with them.

Not all of us can work from home, so I'll share the rule I was taught about wearing sandals to work. My first summer in a law firm I asked a co-worker about wearing open-toed shoes. She said it was only allowed if I had a pedicure, meaning my toenails had to be painted. Only sandals with heels were permitted. I decided to save money on the pedicures and was much more comfortable in closed-toe shoes.

Dressing kids for school

Uniforms are not mandatory in most public schools in the U.S., but there are exceptions. Private schools usually require students to wear uniforms. In both cases, parents must purchase the uniforms.

America is a materialistic society. Clothing is the cause of much teasing and bullying. A co-worker told me her son's grandmother bought him "name brand" sneakers so that the other boys wouldn't ridicule him. These types of sneakers can cost over one hundred dollars. With girls, it can be even worse. Clothing is social currency - those with the right look are likely to fit in. Who defines this right look? Usually advertisers and celebrities.

For children of immigrants, clothing can be a source of embarrassment. My husband told me he didn't wear jeans until middle school. His mother did not think jeans were appropriate for school.

One Indian mother in a wealthy, professional suburb shared a story that speaks to the importance of being aware of clothing customs. Her daughter came home from school one day with the news that there was a new Indian girl in class. This was good news, except that the other kids in class were laughing at the new girl. It seems she was wearing stockings (tights) as leggings (pants). Stocking are generally translucent and worn under other clothing, not as pants. My cousin reached out to the mother and guided her through the confusing and overwhelming world of girls' clothing.

26

SPORTS

 mericans are crazy about sports. Sports is big business, a major revenue source for schools, a way into college and one of the more racially integrated sectors of society.

What are the major sporting events in the U.S.?

Super Bowl - football championship game, played in early February. The most watched annual sporting event in America, with over one hundred million viewers. Even people who hate football watch for the advertisements and the half-time show. However, it is not the most viewed sporting event in the world - just compare the number of viewers to the World Cup (one billion) and Cricket World Cup (two billion).

World Series - baseball championship game played between the top teams from the National League and American League. Playoffs begin in the fall.

. . .

NBA Finals - basketball championship series. The final two teams play a series of seven games to determine the winner. The finals usually begin in May.

Stanley Cup - hockey championship game, played in June. The Stanley cup is the name of the trophy awarded to the winner.

Indy 500 - The Indianapolis "Indy" 500 is a five-hundred mile race for "indycars" participating in the NTT IndyCar Series league. These cars only seat one driver, are open on top and have engines with about 500-700 horsepower. The race happens in Indianapolis, Indiana on Memorial Day weekend (late May).

Daytona 500 - This is the first race for the NASCAR season of car racing. NASCAR cars are known as "stock cars" and are different than indy cars. The race is held in mid-February in Daytona, Florida.

NCAA Tournament - college basketball tournament held every March (also known as "March Madness"). Teams are divided into brackets, and it is common for Americans to pick teams and enter informal "betting pools" for the tournament. The final sixteen teams are the "Sweet Sixteen" and a surprise team advancing in the tournament is a "Cinderella story."

U.S. Open - annual tennis tournament held in Queens, NY. This is one of the four major tennis tournaments - the others are the Australian Open, Wimbledon (UK) and the French Open. The U.S. Open tournament is held at the end of the summer.

· · ·

The Masters - this is perhaps the most well known golf event in the U.S., although the U.S. Open (for golf, not tennis) is a close second. The Masters tournament is played in April at the Augusta National Golf Club in Augusta, Georgia. .

Do Canadian teams play in U.S. leagues?

Canadian teams can be found in baseball, basketball and especially hockey. There are no Canadian teams in the NFL. Canada has its own football league.

Is sports betting legal in the U.S.?

In 2018, the U.S. Supreme Court ruled that states have the power to regulate sports betting - this means states can declare sports betting legal within a particular state. Before the ruling, sports betting was only legal in Las Vegas, casinos and certain online gaming websites. In the near future, you will see states allow sports betting, if only for the reason that they can tax the expected high volume of revenue created by the gambling companies.

What about cricket?

You can find cricket games in cities with high Indian populations, and on the Indian television channels, but other than that not many Americans follow the sport. Say the word "cricket" and they will think you are talking about an insect.

Is soccer popular in the U.S.?

Americans seem to like playing soccer more than watching it. Soccer is very popular on the amateur level. It is usually the first sport kids learn to play, and if you have kids you will no doubt attend a game where five year olds run in a pack after the ball. At these games you will not hear talk about the U.S. professional soccer teams or international teams - unless it is a World Cup year and even then not much attention is given to the sport until the end. This could be because the U.S. is not dominant in international soccer, and we can't take the harm to our national ego.

Why do so many kids play sports in America?

Many American parents have this same question! Also, why start at such an early age and why spend weekends traveling hours to games?

One reason is college. Yes, parents of five year olds are thinking about college. College athletes get into schools they are not academically qualified to attend, and usually get scholarships, too! Why? Because colleges make money from college athletes - ticket sales, sponsorships, television rights, merchandising. We're talking millions of dollars.

A more wholesome reason is to keep children healthy. Other parents say sports "keep the kids out of trouble," which could have some merit. Kids who are concerned about physical fitness and team obligations may have less time to get into trouble.

My husband and I are not natural athletes, and although we played some sports growing up (my father even coached my soccer teams), excelling at sports wasn't emphasized. So we don't emphasize it with our kids, but we do get them involved in sports for one reason I haven't mentioned yet - socialization. Playing sports can help kids learn social lessons like being part of a team, the importance of practice and handling defeat.

Are hunting and fishing considered sports?

Thankfully, they are not Olympic sports and not the type of sports you will find on television or in stadiums. There are hunting and fishing competitions and leagues, but you can easily avoid them if you want to.

· · ·

Is football dangerous?

The science suggests that repeated hits to the head, especially for players who start before the age of twelve, could lead to a condition called CTE - chronic traumatic encephalopathy. This condition is a deterioration of the brain for which there is no treatment or cure. The National Football League (NFL) responded to these research claims by saying it supports research into CTE and has made rule changes to minimize contact with the head, but the research does not confirm that football is a cause of CTE.

It looks like many girls play sports in America, too.

This is true, and something that has changed in a generation. My mother and her peers did not play sports, and were not encouraged to. Today, a girl can play sports and be feminine. Female leagues exist for most sports, including basketball, golf, soccer and tennis. Female athletes such as Danica Patrick (NASCAR racing), Billy Jean King (tennis), Serena and Venus Williams (tennis) and Mia Hamm (soccer) have led the way in changing the view of women in sports.

What is Title IX?

Title IX is part of federal education law that prohibits gender discrimination in an activity that receives federal funding. This law has been used to ensure women are not discriminated against in college athletics. Support for female athletes on the college level has also contributed to the rise of females in professional sports and general acceptance of women in sports.

What if my kids are not good at sports?

I have noticed that for boys, being good at sports is valuable social capital - meaning it makes them cool. The good news is that in America there are plenty of sports to chose from. You can find a sport suited for your child - swimming, fencing, chess, biking, rock climbing, ice skating, gymnastics, track (running), volleyball, sailing - the list is endless.

27

ALCOHOL, DRUGS AND CIGARETTES

A lcohol is not *"daru"* in American culture - it is a huge part of American culture. You can't miss all the alcohol advertisements, the references in television shows and movies, or how often your friends and co-workers "meet up for drinks." Drinking alcohol is so common that it is shortened to the word drink. "Do you drink?" may seem like an obvious question, but they are not asking about water or the basic function needed to stay alive. They want to know if you drink alcohol, and by now you may be wondering how you can refuse alcohol and still be social.

Is it rude to refuse alcohol if it is offered to me?

No. The opposite is true - it is rude to pressure someone to drink. The person offering the drink may be using it to be social - to "share a drink" is a common way to unwind in America. Therefore, simply say you'd like to drink something else, not that you don't want to spend time with the person.

But is a woman who drinks considered less respectable?

This is true for men and women if they abuse alcohol and drink too much. I've heard that drinking in India can hurt a woman's reputation, and one immigrant shared that if he shared pictures online of him drinking his relatives in India would go to the extreme of calling him an alcoholic. A woman who drinks responsibly is not viewed in a negative light in America. It is all about being safe and responsible.

What about drinking at work events?

Drinking runs so deep in American culture that it is even common in the workplace. I have been offered wine at work lunches and dinners, and always offered a drink at office parties, usually by my superiors for a job well done. It can be especially awkward to refuse a drink from your boss.

One female Indian co-worker explained to me that she did not want to refuse, so she accepted the drink and held it during the party without drinking it. This helped her avoid the issue. Another trick she used was to get herself a non-alcoholic drink first, so if anyone offered her a beverage she would say she already had one. She felt it was important to socialize with her work colleagues to hear work stories and build relationships outside of the workplace. Soon she noticed that nobody really cared whether she drank alcohol or not.

What is Alcoholics Anonymous?

This is a well known twelve step program that alcoholics use to overcome their addiction.

What is a DUI?

Driving Under the Influence of drugs or alcohol ("DUI") is a crime and very dishonorable. The societal shame is not because the driver was drinking, but rather because the driver selfishly put other drivers in danger. The blood alcohol level for drunk driving is usually .08%. Cops will stop a driver suspected of drunk driving and use a "breathalyzer" and other tests to determine if the driver is drunk. The government estimates that about 30% of traffic deaths are from drunk driving. It is a major problem connected to the drinking culture in America.

Is marijuana legal in the U.S.?

Marijuana ("pot") is legal in several U.S. states, such as California and Colorado. In some states, only medical marijuana is legal, but in others it can be purchased for non-medical uses.

Even in places where marijuana is illegal, this drug is common in schools and colleges. It is cheap, easily available, and viewed as the least harmful of illegal drugs. Chances are that if you went to any high school student in America and asked how to get pot, they would know where to direct you. The growing acceptance of marijuana could be from legalization in certain states, support from the business community for new "cannabis" companies, and a belief that the drug is recreational (like drinking) and not addictive.

What is the opioid epidemic?

Opioids are highly addictive painkillers prescribed by doctors, such as oxycodone, morphine and hydrocodone. These drugs get into the hands of addicts through the black market or from doctors who overwrite prescriptions for them. Federal and state governments are fighting this epidemic with enforcement (arresting dealers and corrupt doctors) and establishing new rules for the prescription and sale of the drugs. This area is highly regulated, but there are still abuses and many cases of opioid addiction and death.

I see a lot of "No Smoking" signs in America. What is that about?

Smoking cigarettes used to be like drinking in America - advertised everywhere and a big part of the social scene. When I was a kid I remember airplanes had smoking and non-smoking sections, as if it is possible to keep the smoke in one area. We have now learned that second-hand smoke can be just as harmful as smoking the cigarette yourself.

This is why you see so many "No Smoking" signs, and why the number of people who smoke declines every year. Drugs are more of a problem with young people than smoking.

In the 1990's, it became clear that tobacco companies had been lying to the public about the health risks and addictive quality of cigarettes. Over forty states brought suit against the tobacco companies, resulting in a 1998 settlement that ended certain marketing practices and required the companies to compensate states for tobacco-related health costs. The price of cigarettes also increased due to heavy state taxes.

Why didn't the tobacco companies go bankrupt after the 1998 settlement? As the U.S. market shrank, tobacco companies pushed their products in the Middle East, Africa and Asia.

28

GUNS

J ust say the word "gun" in America and you will get vastly different reactions. It is one of the most divisive issues in America, only made worse by the horrifying mass shootings that are now too familiar to Americans.

Is gun ownership legal in the U.S.?

Yes - but this is not the full answer.

The Second Amendment of the Constitution states the following: "A well regulated Militia, being necessary to the security of a free State, the right of the people to keep and bear Arms, shall not be infringed."

When the Second Amendment was written America had just fought a war for independence from an oppressive king. I can understand why the founding fathers did not want the government to "infringe" upon the right of people to defend themselves. What if it was necessary to revolt again? How would people do this without weapons? This distrust and fear of government has lasted to this day, and you will hear it in the gun debate.

Like any right in the Constitution, the right to own a gun is not absolute. This right must be balanced against public safety. This is why Congress and the state have the power to regulate guns. Recently, the House of Representatives passed a bill requiring background checks for all gun sales by any dealer (this goes beyond the current law, which only applies to licensed dealers). It is unlikely to become law because the Republicans control the Senate, and as you will read below, the NRA (National Rifle Association) controls many Republicans.

How do I know if my state has strong gun laws?

This is what you should look for: (1) does the state ban assault weapons and/or semi-automatic weapons; (2) does the state have a gun registry; (3) are there limits on the number of rounds of bullets that can be sold at one time; (4) how extensive is the state's background check process and does it apply to private dealers; and (5) does the state ban open and/or concealed carry.

The states with the strongest gun laws are California, Connecticut, Maryland, New Jersey, New York, Colorado, Hawaii and the District of Columbia.

Do the police carry guns?

Yes.

What is the National Rifle Association (NRA)?

The NRA is the membership and lobbying group that fights against stronger gun control. It donates millions to Republican politicians who block bans on assault weapons and other restrictions. The NRA is financially supported by membership dues, but mostly by gun manufacturers and industries that benefit from weak gun laws. It has also been reported that the NRA receives a percentage of gun sales from some manufacturers. Gun sales keep the NRA going, so it is no surprise that they fight any action that could slow those sales, even if the action would keep people safer.

. . .

Why are there so many mass shootings in America?

A big part of the explanation is the weapon that is used in most of these shootings - an assault weapon (also known as semi-automatic weapon). These are not handguns. These are weapons of war intended for use on battlefields and should not be legal for sale, in my opinion. Under President Clinton, the federal government banned assault weapons and "high capacity magazines" (these allow shooters to keep shooting multiple rounds of ammunition without reloading). In 2004, this law expired and has not been renewed, despite an effort by President Obama after the 2012 school shooting in Newtown, Connecticut. Even when the ban was adopted in 1994, it was by a slim margin of 52-48 votes. Only seven states have a ban on assault weapons. It is a stain on our national conscience that the mass murder of children has not led to a ban on assault weapons.

Are children safe in school?

Since Congress hasn't acted to protect children from assault weapons, local schools have their own safety protocols. Students and teachers go through "active shooter trainings" and students are taught about "stranger dangers." Access to entry is highly restricted, and security officers at some schools carry guns.

What about guns in the home?

Some Americans do keep a gun in the home for protection. Ironically, the stories you hear about these guns involve children shooting them by accident, often with horrific results.

One mother who recently immigrated from the United Kingdom asked me if it is appropriate to ask parents if they keep guns in the home. This question is certainly appropriate, especially if the child's parent is a police officer or veteran.

29

FOOD

When it comes to food, I'm not very patriotic. That's because in my opinion, the best food in American comes from outside America. Italian, Chinese, Mexican, Indian, Japanese food - you can find it all here, thanks to immigrants!

Food is entertainment in the United States. Chefs are celebrities who open multiple restaurants, host television shows, write best-selling books and have millions of fans. You don't have to cook to be a fan - these celebrities are mainstream, household names. Cooking competitions are some of the most popular shows on television. Food websites and blogs are everywhere online.

American parents view cooking as an important life skill. Learning to cook prepares children for living alone, either in college or as young adults. For this reason, you will see cooking classes for kids - boys and girls - cookbooks for kids and kids helping in the kitchen at home.

What if I can't eat American food without adding red pepper flakes or hot sauce?

I can't argue with this one. Traditional American food is short on flavor, and many Americans complain that they can't "handle" spicy food. I guess we are gastronomically weaker than our neighbors to the east!

A perfect example is Thanksgiving dinner - the iconic American meal. It's sacred, right up there with The Last Supper (Jesus' last meal with his disciples, the subject of Leonardo da Vinci's famous painting). You would think such a celebrated meal would be delicious, right?

Let me tell you what happened when my husband joined my family for his first traditional Thanksgiving dinner. He was excited, after years of seeing images of turkeys every November and hearing so much about this classic meal. After his first bite, which I was carefully observing, he shyly asked for the salt. I tell you he must have whispered it to me, but my mother did not miss it.

"Did Nagendra like the food?" she asked me later that night.

I could tell this was incomprehensible to her, almost blasphemy. The prized turkey had received all her love and care. She woke up at dawn to clean and "put the bird in," then checked on it every half hour and gently basted it in its natural juices. You would think it was a newborn baby.

"He's just used to spicy food," I told her.

She was offended - a mistake many Americans make. Why is it that Americans can say they don't like spicy food but Indians can't say they don't like bland American food? The Indians I know laugh when I say something is too *tita*, they do not get insulted. They will even put aside a plate that is less spicy for me. I can't imagine my mom spicing up the Thanksgiving turkey for my Indian husband.

I've seen Indians use red pepper flakes, chili powder and hot sauce on everything from eggs to pizza. So the lesson is, if you are going to a traditional Thanksgiving dinner, maybe sneak some of these flavorings with you, but don't let the cook catch you.

What is the difference between vegetarian, vegan, pescatarian, and gluten free?

Americans love to talk about what they do and don't eat. They also love to name their eating habits, and these names can get confusing. The categories below can be broken down into subcategories and beyond, but I just wanted to give you the basics.

Vegetarian: does not eat any animal or fish, but eats eggs and dairy.

Vegan: Vegetarian, but also doesn't eat any animal products such as dairy and eggs.

Pescatarian: Vegetarian who eats fish.

Gluten free: This diet excludes gluten, which is a protein found in wheat and other grains. This diet helps people with celiac disease, joint pain and gluten sensitivities, but has been adopted by others as well.

Is it hard to be a vegetarian in America?

It is much easier than years ago. Younger Americans are embracing a vegetarian diet for health reasons. A recent Gallup poll found that about 10% of Americans under fifty are vegetarian or vegan. Most restaurants offer vegetarian options. The increasing presence of Indian and other Asian restaurants has also improved eating options for vegetarians.

What is the difference between meat and chicken?

This may sound like a silly question, but for Indians meat and chicken often seem to be the same because beef is not an option in India. "Meat" in America refers to beef and chicken, as well as other animal products.

An Indian immigrant friend shared with me that she thought meat and chicken were interchangeable until one fateful day in her high school Spanish class. The teacher asked her for the Spanish word for meat. Instead of "carne" (meat in Spanish), she said the work "pollo" (chicken in Spanish). She didn't know there were different kinds of meat because the only meat her family ate was chicken.

The class laughed at her mistake. This became a running joke in her school (a "running" joke is a joke that people do not let go - they will still talk about it for years). She laughed along, but felt foolish and lonely inside.

What is the "food pyramid" used for?

The U.S. Department of Agriculture started publishing food guidelines for healthy eating in the early 1900's. It might seem strange for a government agency to set eating standards. When I was a kid, we learned about the "food pyramid" in school. In 2011, the pyramid became "MyPlate." You will probably encounter this guide at the pediatrician's office and your child's school.

Where can I get my favorite Indian foods?

When I married my husband fifteen years ago, his mother had to travel over an hour for an Indian grocery store. Now, not only are there more Indian stores, but the non-Indian grocery stores sell Indian spice mixes and fruits like mango, papaya and pomegranate. Many Indian stores ship out of state, and dry Indian goods can be found on Amazon or other Indian grocery websites.

Why are there so many grocery stores (supermarkets) in America?

Supermarkets are everywhere in America - several in each town and often so big they rise up like food temples. It's no surprise we overeat. As a new immigrant, my mother-in-law was so nervous to enter the huge supermarkets that she would only go with a group of Indian friends.

Walk inside a supermarket and you'll be overwhelmed by choices - ten types of apples, fifteen brands of pasta. It can give you a headache, and you feel like you need a PhD to figure out what to buy. I brought one friend to Walmart shortly after she arrived from

India and all of the shampoo choices made her dizzy! "Just tell me what to get," she said.

Is the food in supermarkets fresh?

Strawberries in winter. Carrots in spring. Whatever the season, you can find whatever you need in American supermarkets. If it is growing anywhere in the world, it can be shipped to American supermarket shelves. As a result, fruits and vegetables are picked too soon and treated with chemicals to preserve freshness as long as possible.

Look for the "grown locally" section of the supermarket, and shop at farmer's markets if there are any nearby. Another trick is to buy frozen fruits and vegetables because they are not treated with preservatives.

Is "organic" food really any different?

"Organic" has become a buzz word in America. These foods are supposed to be free of pesticides and chemicals. However, few of us know what "organic" really means and what the requirements are for using the term on food packaging.

If you see the organic seal, that means the food supplier has complied with the requirements set forth by the U.S. Department of Agriculture. Environmental groups created a list of the "dirty dozen" foods that should be bought organic. The list changes from year to year, but usually includes strawberries, apples, grapes, peaches, spinach, pears, tomatoes, kale.

Food is not the only product that can be organic in America. You will see organic cotton, wool and the phrase "100% Organic" or "Made with 100% Organic Materials" on many types of products. To be honest, you see "organic" listed so much that it has almost lost its meaning.

. . .

Why are Americans staring at food packages before they buy them?

I know it looks odd - a shopper standing in the middle of the supermarket aisle staring at a can of soup or bag of chips.

What is this person doing? Probably reading the food label. Americans have been taught to read food labels. They look for fat, sodium and sugar content, and unhealthy ingredients like high fructose corn syrup.

Food companies are required to list ingredients in order of most to least and what percentage of certain items fulfill the "Recommended Daily Allowance" for a "healthy" person. These terms are defined by another government agency, the National Institutes of Health.

What is fast food?

This is also known as "take out" or "take away" food. Until recently, "fast food" has been quick and cheap, but not healthy. The old timers of fast food are McDonalds, Taco Bell, Kentucky Fried Chicken and Burger King. Pizza is also fast food. Domino's Pizza and Pizza Hut exist in America as they do in India, but you will find that the local pizza place is far superior than these well known franchises.

The fast food that is popular today is also healthy - examples are Panera, Chipotle, sushi and salad bars.

How is breakfast different in India and America?

There is an American saying - "Breakfast is the most important meal of the day." American and Indian breakfasts are very different. This is clear from the troubles facing Dunkin' Donuts in India.

As the Dunkin' Donuts company realized, Indians do not prefer a "grab and go" breakfast. Rather, they eat a sit-down breakfast with family. Unlike Americans, Indians do not consider sugary foods like donuts to be breakfast food. It is also true that Indians are becoming more health conscious and do not want to start the day with high fat, sugary foods.

What is typical American lunch food?

Sandwiches, pizza, burgers, wraps, burritos and salads are popular lunch items, as are leftovers from dinner the previous night.

What is American street food?

These are called "food carts" in America and you don't just find them in cities. In my town there are two food carts - one for hot dogs and another for desserts. But these are nothing compared to the variety and quality of the food carts in cities. The type of food carts reflect the ethnicities living in the cities. For example, in Los Angeles the taco (Mexican) food carts are legendary. In Manhattan, you find Falafel, Indian, German, Greek (gyro), Halal and of course hot dog and pretzel carts. You can find reviews on these carts and even track them online to know when they are close by.

Why are vitamins and supplements so popular in America?

You may have noticed that the traditional American diet is heavy on the carbs and meats, and light on vegetables. Americans want a quick fix for this dietary imbalance, and vitamin supplements are one solution.

Are there more coffee or tea drinkers in America?

Coffee is extremely popular in America. My father used to joke that Americans "worship" their coffee. Americans cradle and caress their coffee cups, and savor every sip.

Tea is also popular, but mostly made at home and not purchased. Not many Americans use loose tea and would not know what to do with it. Making tea is more of an art in India than

America. Americans put milk in their tea after it has brewed, making it less creamy than chai.

Why do Americans use tea bags?

Americans can claim credit for inventing the tea bag...by accident.

An American tea merchant named Thomas Sullivan wanted to send tea to his customers in small sample sizes. He sent the samples of tea to his customers in small silk bags. By mistake, the customers put the silk bags in their cups to brew the tea. They liked the efficiency of the single use bag, so Sullivan tinkered with it and the tea bag was born.

Americans seem really into refrigeration.

This is true. I find myself putting more food items in the fridge than my Indian relatives, and my mom puts even more than me. My mom freezes bread and takes it out to "defrost" when she needs it. Americans worry about food "going bad." You may have noticed there is a "use or freeze by" date on most foods. Most Indians I know ignore these dates.

What is kosher food?

Similar to Jain and other Hindu traditions, Jewish law prohibits cruelty to animals. Kosher means the way the animals are killed and the food is prepared and handled follows Jewish law. There are also prohibited foods, such as shellfish and pork, and milk and meat are not consumed together. Not all Jews "keep kosher." In recent surveys, about a third of Jews follow Kosher eating rules.

30

TRANSPORTATION

A mericans love cars. We used to love big cars, and many still do. But for others, environmental concerns (and the price of gas) have led us to embrace small, energy efficient cars from the Prius to the fully electric Tesla.

What is the highway system?

Roads are managed by the states, but the federal government gives states money for road construction and repair. Towns and cities are connected by the highway system, also known as the Interstate. It is very rare to see a paved road end or turn into a dirt path in America unless there is nothing on the other end of it. You will have to pay tolls for certain roads and bridges, and these are often used to fund maintenance.

Will driving in America be easier than in India?

Yes. Once you learn the rules, driving in America is not hard. You do have to follow the rules, though, or you will get a traffic ticket (fine). Read the signs. Know the speed limit and where you can and can't park.

What if I don't pay a traffic ticket?

These fines will add up and you can lose your license or even be arrested. If you are stopped for another reason and they realize that you have unpaid fines, you can be arrested on the spot. Pay the fine or show up to court to fight it, but don't ignore it.

What about train travel?

America is also connected by a railway system, although long distance train travel is not as popular as flying or driving. There is only one long distance train service - Amtrak - and it is run by the federal government.

Short distance train or subway (underground) travel is very common and run by the states. Millions of American take the train to work, traveling from the suburbs into major cities. Some of the most popular commuting lines are in DC (known as "the metro"), NY ("the subway"), Boston ("the tube") and Chicago ("the L").

Trains and planes generally run on time in America, and when they don't there is always an explanation. The most common reasons for delays are weather and electrical/mechanical problems. It is highly unusual to experience a delay with no explanation. Americans don't just accept delays - they want a reason.

What about scooters?

You will see them in the cities, but not much elsewhere. Motorcycles are more popular in America, especially the legendary "Harley Davidson."

How do I get my driver's license?

You need a driver's license to drive in America. You will need proof of your citizenship or visa status, because in the majority of U.S. states undocumented immigrants cannot obtain a driver's license. The test for the driver's license is handled by the Department of Motor Vehicles. There are two parts to the test - written and driving. Each state decides the age when a person can take the driver's test. If you have a driver's license from your home country, you are eligible for the International Driver's Permit.

What is a "hit and run"?

If you hit another car, don't leave the scene of the accident. This is called a "hit and run." You are expected to stop and get out of the car. The other person will get out as well, but do not be nervous. The other person wants to get your insurance information so that any damage to their car will be paid for by your insurance.

What about the horn?

The car horn is used much less in America than in India. The horn is used to warn other drivers that they are in danger or, for the vengeful types, to tell them they did something wrong. Driving in America is much quieter than in India.

What should I know about buying a car?

Don't go alone. Car salesmen are well known for being very persuasive because they get a commission for the cars they sell. You don't have to buy a new car - dealers also sell pre-owned cars. These are cars that have been leased for a few years, then returned and certified for resale. You don't have to go to the local dealer- you can research prices online and people even travel to different states for the best price.

You need proof of car insurance to purchase a car from a dealer. You also need to register your car with the state, and for that you will need your driver's license and proof of insurance as well.

. . .

What about electric cars?

There is certainly a demand for this technology, and the car companies haven't been able to meet the demand. My husband drives a Tesla, and everywhere we go people ask about it. There are not many car companies that offer a fully electric vehicle, though this will change in the next few years. The government is also supporting the technology by offering tax credits to purchasers of new electric vehicles.

31

HOBBIES

mericans love their hobbies. Crafting, playing in a band, baking, woodworking, running marathons - you would think we have more time than we actually do.

What are popular American hobbies?

Americans enjoy hobbies ranging from bird watching (seriously), knitting and other crafts, gardening (highly popular), reading (for leisure, not required reading), walking (although not as popular as in Europe) and other physical exercise, music, sports and cooking.

Why do Americans collect items like stamps and coins?

These may sound like boring hobbies, but the hope is that over time these "collector's items" will increase in value. Americans can be very nostalgic, and you would be surprised what some pay for old items that appear valueless. In addition to stamps and coins, some other common collector's items are baseball cards, comics, sneakers, watches and old cars.

. . .

What is the Maker Movement?

This global movement celebrates the "do it yourself" mindset. The movement was formalized in 2006 when the magazine *Make* collaborated for the first Maker Faire in San Mateo, California. The Maker Movement has also inspired "maker spaces" where creative thinkers can use materials to tinker and nurture new ideas.

According to the Maker Faire organization, there are forty Maker Faires in cities around the world, and nearly two hundred smaller "mini" Maker Faires in communities worldwide. Unfortunately, there are no Maker Faires in India at this time.

Yoga in America, for real?

You may be thinking, "This is not the yoga I know..." Western-style yoga is definitely different than the yoga in ashrams. The yoga practiced by my father-in-law would be unrecognizable to the ladies at the local yoga studio.

Mainstream American yoga is about stress reduction, mindfulness and physical fitness. There is even such a thing as a "yoga butt." You can find the spiritual message in some classes, but teachers largely stay away from this to keep the practice open to everyone. I have been told by a Christian that some strict Christians consider yoga and meditation to be "worshipping false idols," which is prohibited in the Bible.

In typical American style, there are countless varieties of yoga here. You can try power yoga, yoga-lattes, chair yoga or couples yoga. Take your pick - but don't be disappointed if the only shreds of India left in the practice are the Sanskrit position names!

32

PETS

Pets in America are treated better than some humans in other countries - they have medical care, day care, clothes, toys, special diets and even medication for anxiety. Some call it First World silliness. True, but pets also provide a sense of peace, companionship and purpose that is much needed in our fast-paced, technological culture.

What are common American pets?

Dogs and cats top the list, but it is also common for children to keep hamsters, guinea pigs, birds, snakes and fish as pets.

What are the rules for domesticated animals in the U.S.?

Dogs and cats should be brought to the veterinarian for necessary shots. Dogs must get a rabies shot. Animals are trained and not left to roam the streets. Cat owners can chose whether to keep the cat as an indoor or outdoor cat. Outdoor cats go to the bathroom outdoors and may kill birds and small mice. Indoor cats go to the bathroom in a "litter box" and eat store bought cat food. They never go outside. Cats without owners that live outside are called stray or feral cats.

It is expected for a dog owner to pick up the dog's feces (waste). It some areas leaving the waste is punished by fine. Many people walk their dogs in the neighborhood, and others let the dog out in a fenced area to exercise and go to the bathroom. Either way, it is not acceptable for dog feces to remain on the lawn or streets.

Pet services and resources are easy to find. Many pet stores offer training classes and grooming services. The most important thing to know is that pets require work - they are living things and do not exist for your enjoyment alone. Americans are serious about pet care - pets should be clean, fed, healthy and trained.

What is animal cruelty?

Cruelty to animals is a crime that is punished by fine or jail, depending on the severity. People who are intentionally cruel to animals are considered depraved and immoral. Cruelty to animals is often a sign that the person could commit more violent crimes. Of course, the exceptions are those acceptable forms of cruelty, such as hunting and fishing.

What is animal rescue?

If your friend says she "rescued" an animal, it does not mean she rescued a cat from a tree or a dog from a burning fire. Animal rescue is a term that describes saving an animal from a shelter by fostering or adopting the animal. Animal shelters hold animals that have no owner, and in some shelters unclaimed animals are put to death. It has become popular to "rescue" an animal rather than buy one from a breeder. Rescue animals are usually free and come with the necessary shots.

. . .

What does it mean to have a dog or cat spayed/neutered?

Dog and cat owners are strongly encouraged to have a veterinarian spay/neuter their animals so that they do not procreate. This helps control the pet population and the behavior of the animal as well.

33

HOW AMERICANS VIEW THE WORLD

What I discuss below is the "typical" American view of the world. It is not true for every American. It's also often unintentional. Our world view is the result of geography, wealth, national "myths" we learn in school and our position as an economic and military superpower.

What is the typical American view of the world?

These days, it seems like Americans see their country as the center of the world. It's like the old days before Copernicus and Galileo when humans believed the sun revolved around the Earth.

Americans care about world events when they affect our daily lives. Usually, this is too late. I'm not just talking about crises like climate change, terrorism or political upheaval. No, we aren't paying attention to the good stuff, either. American media covers poverty and rapes in India, not the rising middle class or Bollywood. Americans still think China is one big factory and don't know about "Made in China 2025" or Chinese investments in education and technology.

This is part of the reason why the U.S. is falling behind. Countries are rising all over the world, and we aren't paying attention or learning from them.

What about the Americans who want to save the world?

Some Americans have a "save the world" mentality. These Americans mean well and can have an extraordinary impact on the world. The challenge is that Americans are at risk of bringing their dominant world view to this work. We think we have the answers rather than listening to those we are trying to help.

This isn't just an American problem. It is difficult for anyone to see things from another point of view. The difference is that Americans have the resources and access to actually implement their ideas, forcing others to live with their well intentioned solutions.

This has always been a difficult balance. Even our government is guilty of it, from relations with Native Americans to our "nation-building" efforts in Iraq and Afghanistan. American help comes with the assumption that America knows best. Depending on how badly a country or people need the help, they may not care.

For wealthy and privileged Americans, doing good can be more about feeling and looking good than actually making a difference. Working on issues in other countries can be easier and neater than confronting inequality and poverty back home. We build schools in Africa, but ignore our failing public schools. We help girls in Calcutta brothels, but look away from the sex and labor trafficking in our neighborhoods.

I love the American desire to make the world a better place. I just want us to keep in mind that "better" doesn't mean more like America, and we need to listen first rather than pushing our ideas on others.

How do Americans view other countries?

Again, these are generalizations and do not apply to all Americans. With that said...

Americans still have a teenager/parent relationship with

England. America is the rebellious yet adoring teen. This is why we have so many Anglophiles - people who love everything British. You will see that British culture sells big in America. In music, Americans love British bands like The Beatles, The Rolling Stones and One Direction. British television shows like Downton Abbey are obsessions, and we can't forget the royals. Princess Diana was beloved in the U.S., as is the new princess, American Meghan Markle. Of course, Americans will denounce the idea of royalty, but enjoy the fairy tale of the royal family.

When I returned from my first trip to India, a co-worker asked me, "Did you see many British colonial buildings?" It's the land of the Taj Mahal, and she was asking about British buildings. That's just one example of the American fascination with England.

If England is the older parent, Canada is an ignored sibling and Mexico is a younger sibling that gets dumped on.

You don't hear much about Canada in America. It's strange, since we are neighbors. Before the 2016 election you would hear, "I'm moving to Canada if Trump wins," but not many people really did. These days, Canada's Prime Minister Justin Trudeau is welcoming the immigrants and refugees that America turns away. The ignored sibling is suddenly making us look bad.

Mexico isn't ignored. Almost every week President Trump blames Mexico for the flow of drugs, criminals and undocumented immigrants across the border. During the 2016 campaign, President Trump said Mexico would pay for the border wall. Mexico never agreed to this, and has not caved to President Trump's pressure. From the political talk you may think Mexico is an enemy of the U.S., but the two countries are deeply linked economically and culturally.

Americans have an even worse view of Central America. This is because they do not understand the history of these countries, or the role of the U.S. in creating instability in the region. Americans only see the "caravans" and gangs from Guatemala, El Salvador, Honduras and Nicaragua, and are blind to the reasons driving these immigrants from their homelands.

Then there is Africa. For many Americans, Africa is a land of

AIDS, famine and war. It is rare to find an American who knows the meaning of the "African diaspora" or is interested in taking an honest, serious look at the lasting impact of the slave trade on Africa.

Even with this dark history, Africa is on the rise. Ghana, Ethiopia, the Ivory Coast, Tanzania and Senegal are experiencing rapid economic growth. There are bountiful natural resources, which have often been the reason for conflict and colonization on the continent. Still, the average American doesn't view Africa as a profitable market or trading partner. America has not pursued an aggressive economic strategy in Africa, but China has been building factories and infrastructure and rapidly increasing its trade with Africa.

What about India? How do Americans view India?

I'd say Americans have three views of India. The first is a land of ancient wisdom, the birthplace of Buddhism, Hinduism, yoga and other spiritual traditions. Americans speak of traveling to India and coming back changed, even enlightened.

Then there is the second view - the India of slums, poverty, oppressed women, overcrowded cities and filth. This is often the image of India in the media. My husband jokes that whenever the television show "Amazing Race" goes to India, they always find the worst possible conditions for the contestants.

The third view is from trips to the doctor and customer service. Indians are the largest group of foreign trained doctors in America. Indian doctors have gained the respect of Americans, which translates into a more positive view of India.

Americans also interact with Indian citizens during calls to customer service. No matter how hard these Indians try to learn the American way of speaking, the calls usually end badly. Americans complain about "being connected to someone half way around the world," and are left with the view of Indians as simple folk answering phones at an Indian call center all day.

34

WHAT AMERICANS CAN LEARN FROM INDIAN IMMIGRANTS

U*nderstand how lucky you are to be born in America.*
Almost every Indian immigrant I have interviewed for this book said they came because in America, if you work hard you can succeed. I wish Americans understood that in most places in the world, hard work is just not enough. Hard work doesn't get you anywhere in a corrupt society, a country at war, a country that denies rights to people based on gender, caste, skin color, wealth or political opinions. People come to America because with hard work you can move up, you are not stuck in a position by forces beyond your control.

There are many reasons why some Americans do not understand this. If I hadn't married into an Indian family, I might not understand it myself. Sure, my grandparents were immigrants from Ireland, Scotland and Italy, but that was before I was born and I have no contact with immigrants fleeing those countries today. If I had the childhood of my husband, always helping (and losing his bedroom to) an Indian immigrant, I might understand the struggles immigrants take on just to have a shot at what I had at my first breath.

Some Americans fall too quickly and too easily into the trap of denying others the opportunities we have just because we were lucky to be born Americans. I don't get it. One clear example is President Trump's complaint that America gets people from "shit hole" countries instead of countries like Norway. Hard work is rewarded in Norway; it isn't in the places he's calling "shit hole" countries. We should welcome people who have the resilience and determination to leave those countries. He doesn't see that, and such a complete lack of understanding makes me sad for my country, and worried for our future. Immigrants will find another place to go, maybe Canada, and take their ambition and potential with them.

If you are going to have an opinion on immigration policy, first understand the U.S. immigration system.

An immigrant's life story doesn't begin when they show up in the U.S. If we are going to make informed, effective immigration policy, we have to understand their backstory as well - the reasons why they came, the harsh journey, the sacrifice and fear of returning home. If they came illegally, we should understand the reasons for that, too. We should understand the lengthy and complicated process of becoming a citizen, and how many immigrants want to come to America and can't because of quotas, lotteries, visa restrictions, consulate practices and other barriers.

Education is survival

Most immigrants from poor countries know that education is the way to advance in society, and usually the only way. It is that simple. The "love of learning" is a western, privileged concept in many ways. I've met many Indian immigrants who don't "love" their chosen profession, but they never expected to. They can do what they love when they are not working, if they have time. Education is survival.

Indians are not smarter than Americans, but they are smarter about their approach to education. They know what to study (math, engineering, medicine), and why they are studying it (to enter a secure profession). The Indians who stray from this model are usually wealthy and have already attained a secure place in society. I once asked my sister-in-law why so many Indians study medicine. She told me that in a poor country, there are few jobs, but you always need a doctor.

Resilience

You hear a lot about resilience and grit in America today. From corporate leaders to parents and teachers, there is a concern that we have become "soft" and entitled. If Americans want to learn about resilience and grit, they should spend time with new immigrants.

When my father-in-law purchased a medical practice on eastern Long Island, his colleagues told him he "might as well bury the money in the ground." Nobody thought patients who had never seen an Indian before would trust him as their doctor. He persevered, and won their trust. When he purchased his first real estate investment property, the lawyer for the seller asked repeatedly, and incredulously, if he really had the money. He taught himself how to invest in the stock market - not just invest, but use the tools better known to Wall Street whizzes than a farm boy from India. Sure, he lost on some deals, but as he said repeatedly, "We are not starving."

Most immigrants do whatever they need to do to survive in America. This is after leaving behind loved ones and enduring tragedies we cannot imagine. Highly educated men and women work stocking shelves, as cashiers, drivers, housekeepers and other jobs just to pay the bills, but they have plans. They study at night for licensing and certification exams so that they can practice their skill here. They take on second jobs. They push their kids to study. They always have plans.

35

CONTINUING THE CONVERSATION

The world is always changing, and so should books. I know you have more questions than those answered here, and there are things I got wrong or left out. America Explained will be revised and updated, hopefully annually. Please contact me to share your thoughts, criticisms and suggestions. I would love to hear your story and advice for other immigrants. That's the only way the book can get better and support more immigrants.

You can email me at allisonsinghbooks@gmail.com, or visit my website at allisonsingh.com, where you can sign up to receive updates about future editions of the book and special offers. The book has an Instagram page (@AmericaExplainedBookSeries) and a Facebook page ("America Explained Book Series").

I hope that reading this book helps you feel more welcome in America. For our country to be great, we have to support our immigrants. This book is my effort to do that, and I thank you for reading it.

If you enjoyed this book, a review on Amazon would be greatly appreciated by the author, as it could help others like you discover the book. Thank you!

NOTES

5. Becoming an American - The Immigration System

1. Pew Research Center Fact Tank, "Key Facts about Asian Americans," September 8, 2017, by Gustavo Lopez, Neil G. Ruiz and Eileen Patten.
2. "Bill Aims to End Decades Long Wait for High-Skilled Immigrants," by Stuart Anderson in Forbes, February 15, 2019.

9. Money & Investing

1. Pew Research Center Fact Tank, "Key Facts about Asian Americans," September 8, 2017, by Gustavo Lopez, Neil G. Ruiz and Eileen Patten.

15. Education - Pre-K through High School

1. West Virginia State Board of Education v. Barnette, 319 U.S. 624 (1943).

16. Education - The College Admissions Process

1. The Harvard process is explained clearly in the January 2019 article in The American Prospect by Jerome Karabel titled "Privileging the Privileged: Harvard's Real Problem."

24. Cultural Traditions, Holidays & Celebrations

1. This figure is from a 1960 Gallup poll cited in the article "Don't Forget MLK Jr. was once Denounced as an Extremist," by Jeanne Theoharris, Time Magazine, January 12, 2018.